MT
92
.B37
L5

Lendvai
Bela Bartok: an analysis
of his music

Date Due

Onondaga Community College

Syracuse, New York

BRO
DART   PRINTED IN U.S.A.

Béla Bartók

An analysis of his music

Béla Bartók

An analysis of his music

By Ernő Lendvai

With an introduction by Alan Bush

KAHN & AVERILL
London

First published in England in 1971 by
Stanmore Press Ltd under their associated imprint: Kahn & Averill
Copyright © Ernő Lendvai 1971

Musical examples are quoted by kind permission of Boosey & Hawkes Ltd
and Alfred A. Kalmus Ltd (Universal Edition).
The publishers would like to thank Ates Orga for his assistance in the
preparation of the music examples.

Printed in Great Britain by
Thomas Nelson (Printers) Ltd, London and Edinburgh

SBN 900707 04 6

Contents

Introduction

The publication of this study of the music of Béla Bartók is an important event. Many descriptive analyses of particular works of his have appeared, but here for the first time in the English language is an authoritative and convincing exposition of the theoretical principles which the composer worked out for himself but refrained, as far as is known, from expounding to anyone during his lifetime, either in writing or by word of mouth. Thus we owe both the author and the publisher a sincere debt.

Mr. Ernő Lendvai has disclosed the fact that Béla Bartók, in his early thirties, evolved for himself a method of integrating all the elements of music; the scales, the chordal structures with the melodic motifs appropriate to them, together with the proportions of length as between movements in a whole work, main divisions within a movement such as exposition, development and recapitulation and even balancing phrases within sections of movements, according to one single basic principle, that of the Golden Section. Some such mathematical proportion was first proposed as an aesthetic principle by Chaldeans in the

3rd millennium B.C., taken up by the Greeks two thousand years later and rediscovered during the Renaissance, but never systematically applied to music at any time. (There exists one single string quartet movement by Haydn, composed in length according to Golden Section proportions, but this is more of an intellectual quirk of the composer's than a principled procedure.) Bartók discovered a way of deriving the basic pentatonic intervals A–G–E and the first inversion of the major common chord E–G–C from the Golden Section in its practicable form of Fibonacci's series of whole numbers. From there Bartók proceeded to the establishment of two fundamental scales, described by Lendvai as "diatonic" and "chromatic", containing respectively seven and eight notes inside the octave. Within this framework Bartók applied his theory of "tonal axes" as the basis of tonality.

It is an implied thesis of the book that the pentatonic scales of the earliest folk music, the modes of oriental and medieval art and folk music and lastly, the major and minor scale idiom of European art music of the 17th, 18th and 19th centuries, are stages on the road towards Bartók's complete integration of the deepest fundamentals of tonality with perfect formal proportion.

During the past fifty years there have been various scientifically orientated attempts within musical theory to show the way forward to the composer and to help him to find a firm foothold in the period of chaos which followed the disintegration of the major and minor scale period at the beginning of this century. The most important in order of their appearance have been Asaviev's "Musikalnaya Forma kak Protsess" and "Intonatsia" (1930), Hindemith's "Craft of Musical Composition" Vol. 1 (English Ed. 1937), Deryck Cooke's "The Language of Music" (1959) and Ernest Ansermet's "Les Fondements de la Musique dans la Conscience Humaine" (1961). To these major works should now be added Lendvai's exposition of Bartók's musical theories. Though these five works

viii

propagate theories which are mutually contradictory in one respect or another, they are all in agreement on one fundamental proposition, namely, that tonality, that tonal relations of some kind or another are an essential framework for any construction of tones which can be rightly considered as a work of musical art. Asaviev's concept of "intonation", Hindemith's "Series 1", Cooke's "pinpointing of the inherent emotional characterisation of the major, minor and chromatic scales",* Ansermet's exposition of the space between the notes making up the octave as a "structured space, divided unequally at the perfect fifth and perfect fourth", and now Bartók's tonal axes, operating within his particular "diatonic" and "chromatic" scales (the latter not the chromatic scale of twelve semitones) are all based upon the admission that there exists a hierarchy of intervals, proceeding from the essential nature of musical tones themselves, which may not be disregarded if music is to result from composing or the putting together of tones.

Some readers may wonder why I have not included among the important theoretical writings of this century Arnold Schoenberg's essay entitled "Composition with Twelve Tones" (1941), the argumentation of which in support of his method of composing with twelve tones which are related only with one another (now known as serial dodecaphony) advances it, in the author's opinion, "to the rank and importance of a scientific theory".** A study of the theoretical paragraphs of this essay dispels any such illusion. The whole justification of the method of composing with twelve tones depends upon the following two sentences:

> "The term emancipation of the dissonance refers to its comprehensibility, which is considered equivalent to the consonance's comprehensibility. A style based on this

---

* Cooke: *The Language of Music*, page xii.
** Schoenberg: *Style and Idea*, page 109.

premise treats dissonances like consonances and renounces a tonal centre."*

Of course dissonance is equivalent to consonance in the sense that both are perfectly permissible ingredients of musical art. But dissonance is not the same as consonance; it has different acoustical and physiological effects. Therefore dissonance ought not to be treated as if it were identical with consonance. And in any case the renunciation of a tonal centre does not follow from any previously stated proposition and is merely a dogmatic assertion of the composer's belief. As such it is totally without the scientific validity which he claims for it, and therefore his essay hardly merits inclusion among the important theoretical writings which are mentioned above.

As far as I am aware no supporter of atonality, serial or otherwise, has provided any proof of its theoretical validity as a possible framework for musical art. The formidable champion of the Vienna School of this century, Theodor Wiesengrund Adorno, in his "Philosophie der neuen Musik" (1948) assumes that, apart from Bartók and Stravinsky, only Schoenberg, Berg and Webern and their followers are worthy to be taken seriously as composers of present-day music. He accepts Schoenberg's justification of his method of composing without comment, as does Josef Rufer in his "Composition with Twelve Notes", but in comparing the Viennese School of the 20th century with the Vienna classics, even he assesses its short-comings very objectively and describes the large works of Schoenberg's mature period as "Werke des grossartigen Misslingens",** which could be literally translated as "works of magnificent failure". If Adorno is unable to justify atonal music, it is needless to add that from the point of view of serious musical theory, the pretentious chit-chat of Mr. John Cage is not worth a moment's consideration.

* Schoenberg: *Style and Idea*, page 105.
** Adorno: *Philosophie der neuen Musik*, page 96.

In conclusion, the publication of Ernő Lendvai's book can only be welcomed. It should be studied, not only by all Bartók's admirers, together with the other treatises above-mentioned, but by all students of composition who are trying to fight their way out of the present state of confusion in the musical world, and thus to build a framework for their creative work, which is not a chance mixture of the latest styles at present in vogue among one or other small clique, but a logically integrated development from the musical art of past periods. In this fight the struggle of Bartók as expounded by Lendvai, is an inspiration, even if his solution may not be the one which proves to be the most widely accepted.

Alan Bush, Radlett, 1971.

Tonal Principles

The Axis System

"Every art has the right to strike its roots in the art of a previous age; it not only has the right to but it must stem from it", Bartók once declared.

His tonal system grew out of functional music. An uninterrupted line of evolution can be followed from the beginnings of functional concepts, through the harmonies of Viennese classicism and the tone-world of romanticism to his *axis system*.

By an analysis of his compositions, this axis system can primarily be shown to possess the essential properties of classical harmony, i.e.

(*a*) the functional affinities of the fourth and fifth degrees
(*b*) the relationship of relative major and minor keys
(*c*) the overtone relations
(*d*) the role of leading notes
(*e*) the opposite tension of the dominant and subdominant
(*f*) the duality of tonal and distance principles

(*a*) To begin with, let us try to situate Bartók's tonal system in the circle of fifths. Let us take C as the tonic (T). Then F, the fourth degree, is the subdominant (S); G, the fifth degree, is the dominant (D); A, the sixth degree and relative of the tonic, functions as a tonic; D, the second degree, and relative of the subdominant, functions as a subdominant; E, the third degree and relative of the dominant, functions as a dominant. The series of fifths, F–C–G–D–A–E corresponds to the functional series S–T–D–S–T–D.

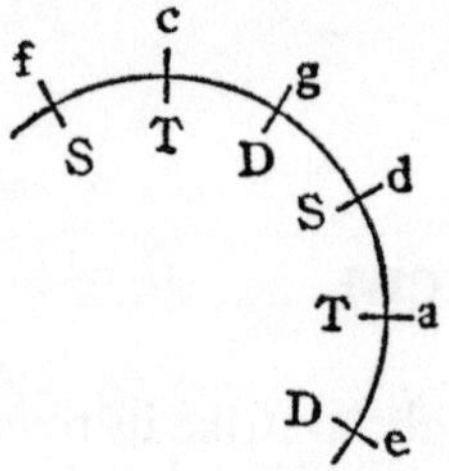

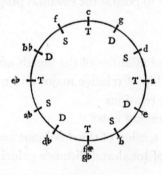

FIG. I

We note that the sequence S–T–D repeats itself. When this periodicity is extended over the entire circle of fifths the scheme of the axis system may be clearly seen:

FIG. 2

2

Let us separate the three functions and call them tonic, sub-dominant and dominant axes, respectively.

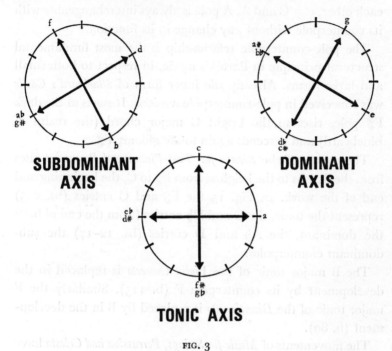

SUBDOMINANT AXIS

DOMINANT AXIS

TONIC AXIS

FIG. 3

Chords based on the fundamental C, E♭ (=D♯), F♯ (=G♭) and A have a *tonic* function.

Chords based on the fundamental E, G, B♭ (=A♯), C♯ (=D♭) have a *dominant* function.

Chords based on the fundamental D, F, A♭ (=G♯), B have a *subdominant* function.

It is essential that the particular axes should not be considered as chords of the diminished seventh, but as the functional relationships of four different tonalities, which may best be compared to the *major-minor* relations of classical music (e.g. C major and A minor, E♭ major and C minor).

3

It should be noted, however, that a much more sensitive relationship exists between the *opposite* poles of an axis—the "counterpoles", e.g. C and F♯—than those situated next to each other, e.g. C and A. A pole is always interchangeable with its counterpole without any change in its function.*

The pole-counterpole relationship is the most fundamental structural principle in Bartók's music, in respect to both small and large forms. Already the inner form of *Bluebeard's Castle* was conceived in pole-counterpole tensions. It starts at the dark F♯ pole, rises to the bright C major chord (the realm of Bluebeard) and descends again to the gloomy F♯.

The course of the *Sonata for Two Pianos and Percussion* rises from the depths to the heights: from F♯ to C, the beginning and end of the work. In Fig. 15 the F♯ and C entries (bs. 2–5) represent the tonic, the G and D♭ entries (from the end of b. 8) the dominant, the A♭ and D entries (bs. 12–17) the sub-dominant counterpoles.

The B major tonic of the *Violin Concerto* is replaced in the development by its counterpole F (b. 115). Similarly the F major tonic of the *Divertimento* is replaced by B in the development (b. 80).

The movements of *Music for Strings, Percussion and Celesta* have the following structure:

MOVEMENT	BEGINNING	MIDDLE	END
I	A	E♭ (b. 56)	A
II	C	F♯ (b. 263)	C
III	F♯	C (b. 46)	F♯
IV	A	E♭ (b. 83)	A

* A cadence-like sequence of chords, E–A–D–G–C–F in the system of Bartók can also be visualised in the following way: E–A–A♭–D♭–C–F, the original D and G being replaced by A♭ and D♭, their counterpoles.

At the very end of *Music for Strings, Percussion and Celesta* (Mov. IV bs. 276–282), we hear instead of F♯^{7}–B^7–E^7–A^7–D^7–G^7–C^7–F^7 the sequence F♯^{7}–B^7–E^7–A^7–G♯^{7}–C♯^{7}–(C^7)–F^7.

4

This table teaches yet another lesson. All four movements rest on the tonic axis, A–C–E♭–F♯. Thus the first and fourth movements are supported by the "principal branch", A and E♭; the middle movements, however, by the "secondary branch", C and F♯. Thus each axis has a two-fold affinity depending on whether we oppose the pole with the counter-pole, or the principal branch with the secondary branch.

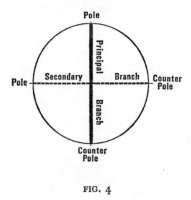

FIG. 4

Consequently the components of the axis system are as follows:

pole	—	(no dimension)
branch	= pole+counterpole	(1 dimension)
axis	= principal+secondary branch	(2 dimensions)
axis system	= T+D+S axes	(3 dimensions)

The Slow Movement of the *Sonata for Two Pianos and Percussion* is based on the subdominant axis, B–D–F–A♭, complying with the traditions of classical composition. The modal arrangement of its principal theme is symmetrical: the beginning and end supported by the B and F counterpoles (i.e. the *principal* branch of the axis), whereas the second and fourth melodic lines rest on the D and A♮ counterpoles (i.e. the *secondary* branch of the axis) with the answer of the changing-fifth (E) in the middle.*

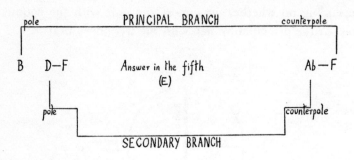

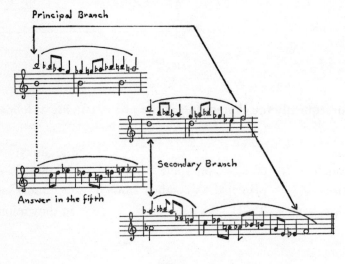

FIG. 5

* The answering lower fifth in which the second section repeats the melody of the first section, is a characteristic of the old-type Hungarian (Cheremiss, etc.) folk song with a descending melodic line. See first example of Fig. 76.

The melody constituting the core of the movement is also centred around the subdominant axis. The G♯ opening and close are replaced in the middle of the theme by the counterpole D. Every main metric and motivic point revolves around the subdominant axis.

FIG. 6

These two melodies truly reflect the structure of the movement, one of them being attached to the principal B–F, the other to the secondary G♯–D branch of the subdominant axis.

The second theme of the *Violin Concerto*, the famous *Reihe* seems to be somewhat more intricate. Although the twelve-tone melody touches every degree of the chromatic scale, there is no doubt as to its tonality. In its axis we see the A and D♯ counterpoles (beginning, middle, end) and the broken-up F♯ major and C major–minor counterpoles.

FIG. 7

7

For further details, see App. I, p. 99.

(*b*) A survey of the evolution of harmonic thinking leads to the conclusion that the birth of the axis system was a historical necessity, representing the logical continuation (and in a certain sense the completion) of European functional music. It can be demonstrated that the axis system, with its characteristic features had, in effect, been used by the Viennese "Greats". Indeed, it had been recognised by Bach, in his chromaticism.

The sense of *functional* correlation in music was introduced in practice by the realisation of the I–IV–V–I affinity (in medieval modal music, at first in cadence form only) In the case of the C tonic:

SUBDOMINANT	TONIC	DOMINANT
F	C	G

The classical theory of harmony already speaks of primary and secondary triads inasmuch as the C may be replaced by its relative A, the F by its relative D and the G by its relative E.

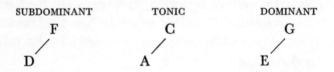

Romantic harmony goes still further, making frequent use of the upper relatives. (Naturally only major and minor keys of similar key-signature may be regarded as relatives, e.g. C major and A minor, or C minor and E♭ major):

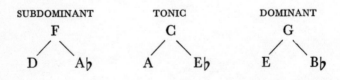

8

One more step completes the system. The axes extend the application of relatives to the *whole* system. The axis system implies the recognition of the fact that the common relative for A and E♭ is not only C, but also F♯ (=G♭); that D and A♭ not only have F as a common relative, but also B; and that E and B♭ not only have G, but also C♯ (=D♭) as common relatives.

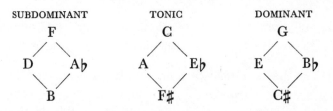

As is well known, Bartók showed a preference for the use of so-called major-minor chords (see Fig. 32b). For instance, its form in C tonality is:

FIG. 8

The function remains unchanged even if the C major mode—as shown in the above chord—is replaced by the relative A minor, or when the E♭ major tonality replaces the relative C minor. This technique occurs regularly in Bartók's music:

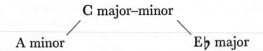

These substitute chords may also be employed in major–minor form, which brings the system to a *close*, since the relative of A major (F♯ minor) and that of E♭ minor (G♭ major) meet at a point of enharmonic co-incidence, F♯=G♭.

9

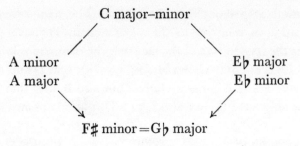

C major–minor

A minor   E♭ major
A major   E♭ minor

F♯ minor = G♭ major

These relatives, applied to dominant and subdominant harmony, again result in the scheme of the axis system.*

(c) The theory of the axis system is also substantiated by the laws of acoustics. Acoustically, arriving from the *dominant* to the *tonic*, is to reach the root from an overtone—all cadential relations rest on the principle of interconnection between roots and their overtones. Thus, the dominant of C is not only G but also the next overtones E and B♭. Therefore the circle of tonic-

---

* One could easily be baffled by the fact that the chord on the seventh degree (B–D–F) assumes a dominant function in traditional harmony. However, in Riemann's opinion, this is but an incomplete seventh chord on the fifth degree. This ambiguity is resolved as soon as either a major or minor chord is based on the B instead of a diminished triad, i.e. the B is granted an independent role. In this case B will have the function of the subdominant. For example, in Beethoven's G major Piano Concerto, the F♯ major chord of the principal theme (b.7) really calls for a subdominant, i.e. a changing dominant interpretation. The difference between the seven-note and the twelve-note systems is conspicuous also in that the circle of fifths built on the notes of the major scale (F–C–G–D–A–E–B) suffers a break between the B and F. No such break occurs in the twelve-note system as it is built up of *homogeneous* interval relations. Were it otherwise then even the simplest relatives—the C major and A minor relationship—would be effected by the contradiction that the chord based on B is undoubtedly of a subdominant character in the A minor key. The same applies to the C♯=D flat degree. It is known from Rameau that the Neapolitan sixth cannot be regarded as a real chord on the second degree; it is not a chord based on D♭, but an altered fourth degree. Also the minor sixth degree in the minor scale could receive a tonic significance by assimilation to the major scale. In an homogeneous twelve-note system, however, these diatonic "transpositions" lose their ground.

dominant relationships is expanded to include E→C and B♭→C.

Since the D–T relationship corresponds* relatively to
the T–S and
the S–D relationship,
overtone–root attraction exists between the T–S and the S–D, as well.

ROOT	OVERTONE		RESULTANT
tonic C	E and B♭	=	dominant
dominant E	G♯ and D	=	subdominant
dominant B♭	D and A♭	=	subdominant
subdominant A♭	C and G♭	=	tonic
subdominant D	F♯ and C	=	tonic

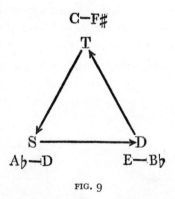

FIG. 9

* The dominant of the dominant (changing dominant) acquires the significance of the subdominant while the dominant of the subdominant assumes the role of the tonic.

11

If we add the role of the nearest overtone, i.e. the fifth, then we can deduce the complete axis system from these relations.

(*d*) In the simplest cadence, that of V⁷–I, the main role is played by the so-called sensitive notes which produce the pull of the dominant towards the tonic. The leading note pulls to the root and the seventh towards the third degree of the tonic, i.e. the leading note B resolves on C and the seventh F on E or E♭.

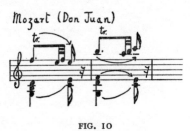

FIG. 10

These important sensitive notes bear a *tritonic* relationship to each other. The tritone—half the octave interval—is characterised by the interchangeability of its notes without changing the interval. Thus, if the B–F relationship is converted into an F–B one (as is frequently the case with Bartók), then the F (=E♯) assumes the role of the leading note, pulling towards the F♯ instead of E, while the seventh B pulls towards A♯ or A instead of C. So, instead of the expected tonic C major, the *counterpole*, the equally tonic F♯ major (or minor) emerges.

FIG. 11

This resolution is reserved by Bartók for a sudden change of scene. The circumstances of an expected G⁷–C cadence emerging as G⁷—F♯ gives us a "Bartókean pseudo-cadence".

(*e*) Starting from the tonic centre C we reach the dominant in one direction and the subdominant in the other, in *identical* latitudes. At a distance of a fifth we find the dominant G upwards and the subdominant F downwards. Regarding *overtone* relations we also get the dominant G, E, B♭ in the upper and the subdominant F, A♭, D in the lower directions.

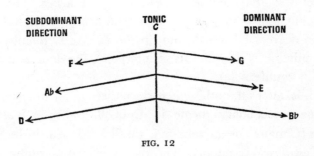

FIG. 12

But what happens if the pendulum covers the latitude of a tritone? In this case the deviations made upwards and downwards meet, both ending at F♯ (=G♭), and if we were to take one as the dominant, then the other would have to assume the subdominant function. By this coincidence, however, a neutralisation of their functions takes place, dominant and subdominant merging are rendered ineffective in the interaction of their opposite forces. Consequently the balance is saved, and the function is invariably that of the tonic. The counterpole is born.

Similarly the distance between the tonic C and F♯ is bisected by E♭ (=D♯) in the one and by A in the other direction; so lying in tensionless, neutral section points, they also have to be interpreted as tonics. No more than four tonic poles can be surmised, since the intervals C–E♭, E♭–F♯, F♯–A, A–C provide no further points of bisection.

Finally, what significance should be attached to a swing of a chromatic degree, of C→B and its counterpart C→C♯ (=D♭)? Which is then to assume the dominant and which the subdominant function? Related to B, C♯ shows a degree of elevation of two fifths, which might correspond to the S–D interdependence, but not to its opposite. Anyway, the subdominant function of B and the dominant function of C♯ are unquestionable when they are related to the tonic F♯ counterpole.

(f) Thus, observing the logic of functional interconnection of the *three axes*, another interesting point arises. The subdominant and dominant are represented most effectively *not* by the degrees IV and V but, in the case of C tonality, the subdominant by A♭ (and its counterpole), the dominant by E (and its counterpole).

This is, after all, nothing new since there is, for instance, the dominant secondary theme in E of Beethoven's *Waldstein Sonata* (C major) or the subdominant Slow Movement in A♭ of the *Pathetique* (C minor). The movements of Brahms' *First Symphony* have the following key-sequence: C–E–A♭–C in the sense of tonic–dominant–subdominant–tonic, etc.

However, the above examination of the axis system fails to explain why Bartók *prefers* these augmented triad relations to the traditional I–IV–V–I. (For examples, see App. II, p. 103.) This necessitates a new approach to the system.

It is generally accepted that twelve-tone music shows a strong tendency to indifferent tonal relations.

Atonal relations can be most suitably effected by the *equal* division of the octave, or of the circle of fifths. By dividing the octave in twelve equal parts we get the chromatic scale; in the case of six equal parts we have the whole-tone scale; four equal parts gives us the chord of the diminished seventh; three the augmented triad, and finally by dividing the octave into two equal parts we arrive at the tritone.

For the present we shall exclude the whole-tone scale because of its limited possibilities: two whole-tone scales produce the chromatic scale by interlocking.

Every tonal system presupposes a centre as well as subordinate relations dependent on the centre. Taking again C as the tonic centre, the three functions are represented most potently by those degrees dividing the circle of fifths into three equal parts, i.e. in the augmented triad C–E–A♭. Properties inherent in classical harmony are responsible for the E assuming a dominant function and A♭ a subdominant function in relation to the tonic C.

Each of these main notes permit their substitution by their counterpoles, i.e. their tritonic equivalents. Thus, C may be replaced by F♯, E by B♭ and A♭ by D.

If we divide the twelve-tone chromatic scale proportionally between the three functions, each function will have four poles, and these—insofar as we keep to the distance principle—are arranged in diminished-seventh relations, dividing the circle into four equal parts. Accordingly, C–E♭–F♯–A belong to the range of the C tonic, E–G–B♭–C♯ to that of the dominant E main note, and A♭–B–D–F to that of the subdominant A♭ main note.

So, the tonal system resulting from a division of the chromatic scale into equal parts agrees completely with the axis system:

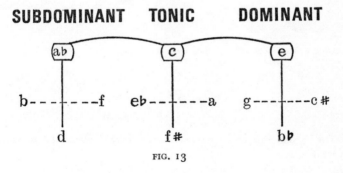

SUBDOMINANT TONIC DOMINANT

FIG. 13

Put concisely, given the twelve-tone system and the three functions this is the *only* system that can be realised by means of distance division.

Viewed historically, the axis system reflects the age-old struggle between the principles of *tonality* and *equi-distance*, with the gradual ascendancy of the latter which finally resulted in the free and equal treatment of the chromatic twelve notes.*
Here we have to draw a line between Bartók's twelve-tone system and the Zwölftonmusik of Schönberg. Schönberg annihilates and dissolves tonality whereas Bartók incorporates the principles of harmonic thinking in a perfect synthesis. To penetrate into Bartók's creative genius is to discover the natural affinities and intrinsic possibilities, inherent in the musical material.

* The introduction of the tempered scale marked about the middle of this road.

Form Principles

Golden Section

Golden Section ("sectio aurea", and henceforth GS) means the division of a distance in such a way that the proportion of the whole length to the larger part corresponds geometrically to the proportion of the larger to the smaller part, i.e. the larger part is the *geometric mean* of the whole length and the smaller part. A simple calculation shows that if the whole length is taken as unity, the value of the larger section is 0.618 . . .

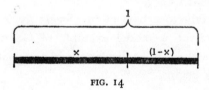

FIG. 14

$$1 : x = x : (1-x)$$

(see upper formula on page 78), and hence the smaller part is 0.382 . . .

Thus, the larger part of any length divided into GS is equal to the whole length multiplied by 0·618 . . .

Bartók's method, in his construction of form and harmony, is closely connected with the law of the GS. This is a formal element which is at least as significant in Bartók's music as the $2+2$, $4+4$, $8+8$ bar periods or the overtone harmonisation in the Viennese classical style.

As an example, let us take the first movement of the *Sonata for Two Pianos and Percussion*. The movement comprises 443 bars, so its GS—following the above formula—is $443 \times 0 \cdot 618$, i.e. 274, which indicates the centre of gravity in the movement: the recapitulation starts precisely at the 274th bar.

Movement I of *Contrasts* consists of 93 bars, and its GS ($93 \times 0 \cdot 618$) again marks the beginning of the recapitulation in the middle of bar 57.

Movement I of the *Divertimento* consists of 563 triplet units (the number of bars is irrelevant owing to their variable time-signatures). The GS of 563 ($563 \times 0 \cdot 618 = 348$) again coincides with the recapitulation.

In Vol. VI of *Mikrokosmos* the GS of "Free Variations" can be seen to touch the "Molto piu calmo"—$82 \times 0 \cdot 618 = 51$.

The GS of "From the Diary of a Fly" comes at the climax: the double sforzando (if the $3/4$ is taken as a $1\frac{1}{2}$ bar, calculating in $2/4$ bars). In "Broken Chords" we find the recapitulation at the GS ($80 \times 0 \cdot 618 = 49$), etc.

The 16 introductory bars of the *Sonata for Two Pianos and Percussion* represent a model example of GS construction— or more precisely, bs. 2–17, because it is here that the organic life of the work begins.

FIG. 15

Its first part is in the sphere of the tonic (bs. 2–5), the second within the dominant (bs. 8–9) and the third part in that of the subdominant (b. 12 on). This third part is thematically the *inversion* of the first two. So, to summarise:

Theme in *root* position—tonic: F♯—C   entries
Theme in *root* position—dominant: G—D♭   ,,
Theme *inverted*—subdominant: A♭—D   ,,

Considering the changes of time-signature, it is more practical to calculate in units of 3/8 time. The whole form consists of 46 units. Its GS is $46 \times 0.618 = 28$, and this covers that part up to the *inversion* of the theme (see the main section of Fig. 16). It can be observed that GS always coincides with the *most* significant turning point of the form.

Let us now separate from the whole the parts in root position, i.e. the first 28 units. Now $28 \times 0.618 = 17.3$. At this very point the tonic part ends—at the first third of the 18th unit (see the dominant entry in Fig. 16).

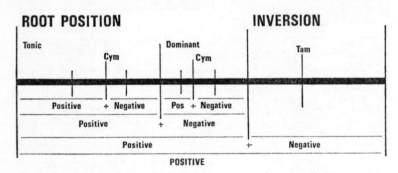

FIG. 16

GS division may be seen to follow one of two possible courses, depending on whether the longer or the shorter section comes first. Let us call one of the possibilities *positive*: long section followed by the short one—and the other *negative*: short section followed by the long one.

In the structure of both tonic and dominant parts the cymbal-stroke creates a sharp duality. The position of the cymbal-strokes is in both cases determined by the GS, but whereas the tonic unit (at the sign "cym" in Fig. 16) is divided so as to make it *positive* ($17 \cdot 3 \times 0 \cdot 618 = 11$), the dominant part, on the contrary, becomes a *negative* division (it consists of 10 units and is divided $4 + 6$). The positive and negative sections complement each other as something with its own mirror-image. But the meeting-point of the two (the dominant entry) has a positive sign.

In other words, condensation and dispersal of the nodes cause a longitudinal undulation, the wave-crests meeting in a *positive* section. Its *negative* counterpart is found at the entry of the tam-tam (in the inversion) so that the positive section of the root and the negative section of the inversion are again joined symmetrically.

Not only the entire formal arc but even the form-cells submit entirely to the strictest geometric analysis. For instance, in the dominant part, we find up to the cymbal-stroke, eleven eighth-notes. Its positive GS point ($7 + 4$) determines the position of the only musical stress in the unit—by means of elongating the E♭ note. This is soon counter-balanced by the negative section-point, at the side-drum beat, in bars 10–11.

Similarly, the positive section of the tonic part up to the cymbal-stroke is marked by the most important turning-point, by the third (C♯) timpani entry—counted in eighths: $33 \times 0 \cdot 618 = 20$. Precisely here, the thematic condensation begins: also, with the 21st eighth. On the other hand, the complementary, negative section of the part following the cymbal-stroke is indicated again by the side-drum (see Fig. 16).

Summarising the above, both in the smaller and larger form-details, there is a symmetric joining of the *positive* and *negative* sections. From these concatenations a single great "potential" form arises, wherein the smaller parts are finally summarised in a *positive* main section. This process is therefore coupled with a powerful dynamic increase, from pianissimo to forte-fortissimo.

Analytical studies permit the conclusion that the positive section is accompanied by intensification, dynamic rise or concentration of the material, while the negative section by a falling and subsiding. The sections always follow the contents and form-conception of the music.

By way of illustration let us subject Movement III of the *Sonata for Two Pianos and Percussion* to a detailed analysis. Exemplary, is the unity of proportions of the exposition: the principal theme has a positive and the closing theme a negative section, while the secondary theme developed between the two is symmetrically arranged.

Thus, the principal theme* (43·5 bars long) is divided as follows: $A_1 + A_2 + B$. The position of B is determined by: $43·5 \times 0·618 = 27·5$, while the two A's are related to each other according to: $27·5 \times 0·618 = 17$.

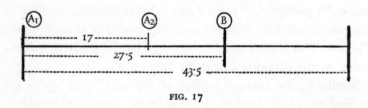

FIG. 17

* The incomplete half-bar at the beginning of the movement is to be taken into consideration when making these calculations.

The symmetrical division of the secondary theme can be expressed as following: $12 + 17\cdot5 + 17\cdot5 + 12$ (bs. 44–102). The geometrical centre (b. 73) accords with the tonal construction of the theme also.

The negative main section of the closing theme (bs. 103–133) is given in b. 115 (see Fig. 18). Within this, bs. 115–133 have a positive section in b. 127 because of the powerful dynamic ascent, and the static construction in $4 + 4 + 4$ units of bs. 103–114 produces a solid base for this rise.

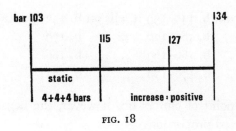

FIG. 18

Likewise the proportions of the development are symmetrical (bs. 134–247).

Its negative main section—counterbalancing the positive main section of the development of Movement I—is determined precisely by the point of climax in b. 177 (F♯ tonic counter-pole).

The *positive* section of the part preceding the climax and the *negative* section after the climax indicate the most important turning points: b. 160 the fugato of the principal theme, while b. 205 the return of the first theme of the development (xylophone entry):

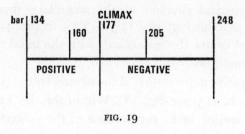

FIG. 19

The build-up towards the climax is always marked by a positive section:

  from b. 140–159 it falls on b. 152 (positive)
   ,,   b. 160–176   ,, ,,   b. 170   ,,
   ,,   b. 160–169   ,, ,,   b. 166   ,,
   ,,   b. 170–176   ,, ,,   b. 174   ,,

From the point of climax on, however, the negative sections show inverted proportions:

  from b. 177–204 it falls on b. 189 (negative)
   ,,   b. 189–204   ,, ,,   b. 195   ,,
   ,,   b. 195–204   ,, ,,   b. 199   ,,

The climax itself is divided statically into 6+6 bars (bs. 177–188).

 The negative main section of the recapitulation (bs. 248–350) coincides with the watershed, as it were, of the thematic material, i.e. with b. 287. Bs. 287–350 form one single broad wave, and its structural view is similar to that of the beginning of Movement I (cf. Fig. 16):

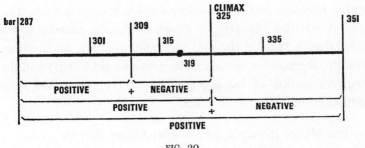

FIG. 20

The negative main section of the coda* (bs. 351–420) coincides with the thematic centre of gravity of the whole coda: at the same time the return of the C tonic, in b. 379, is given a greater emphasis by a lengthy preparation. Corresponding to its static structural character this thematic centre has an 8+8 bar division (bs. 379–394).

The first part of the coda (bs. 351–378) combines a positive

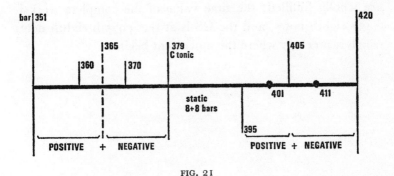

FIG. 21

* N.B. The last index of bars in the score (411) is erroneous.

25

and a negative section in units of $9+5$ and $5+9$ bars. The second part (bs. 379–420), as shown in Fig. 21, contains at the same time a positive (b. 405) *and* a negative (b. 395) section. Finally, the positive section of bs. 395–404 (in b. 401) and the negative section of bs. 405–420 (in b. 411) are again symmetrically related to each other.

At first glance it may appear contradictory that the points of section determined by the laws of GS can remain *unaffected* by the changing tempi. This phenomenon is easy to understand if we consider that music breathes in metric pulsation and not in the absolute measurement of time. In music, passing time is made realisable by beats or bars whose role is more emphatic than the duration of performance. Subjectively we feel time elapse more feverishly in a movement with a quick time-beat and more sluggishly in a slow pulsation.

Finally, let me give an example to those who reproach Bartók for not having effected the "total and radical reorganisation of the material". The complete form of the *Sonata for Two Pianos and Percussion* is divided into "slow–fast + slow–fast" movements. The GS may therefore be expected to appear at the beginning of the second slow movement. Our expectations are wholly fulfilled; the time value of the complete work is 6,432 eighth notes, and the GS is at the 3,975th eighth note: which is precisely where the movement begins.

Fibonacci Series

All of us who have played *Allegro Barbaro*, have been troubled by the F♯ minor throbbing, extending over 8 or 5 or 3 or even 13 bars. The proportion of

$$3:5:8:13$$

contains a GS sequence, approximately expressed in natural numbers: the *Fibonacci numbers*. A characteristic feature of this sequence is that every member is equal to the sum of the two preceding members:

$$2, 3, 5, 8, 13, 21, 34, 55, 89 \ldots$$

and further, it approximates more and more to the irrational key-number of the GS* (the GS of 55 is 34, and that of 89 is 55).

Let us compare this sequence with the proportions of the fugue (first movement) of *Music for Strings, Percussion and Celesta*. Starting pianissimo it gradually rises to forte-fortissimo, then again recedes to piano–pianissimo. The 89 bars of the movement are divided into sections of 55 and 34 bars by the peak of this pyramid-like movement. From the point of view of colour and dynamic architecture the form sub-divides into further units:

* The square of every number is equal to the product of the preceding and ollowing numbers, plus or minus one.

by the removal of the mute in the 34th bar, and its use again in the 69th bar. The section leading up to the climax (b. 55) shows a division of 34 + 21, and that from the climax onwards, 13 + 21. Thus, the longer part comes first in the rising section, while in the falling section it is the shorter part that precedes the longer, so the section-points tend towards the climax. Positive and negative sections fit together like the rise and fall of a single wave.*

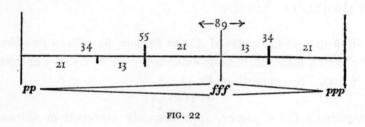

FIG. 22

The proportions follow the Fibonacci series.

It is no accident that the exposition ends with the 21st bar and that the 21 bars concluding the movement are divided into 13 + 8.

The proportions of Movement III of *Music for Strings, Percussion and Celesta* also reflect the Fibonacci series (if we calculate throughout in 4/4 bars and consider the occasional 3/2 as 1½ bars). Its formal and corresponding geometrical structure is shown in Fig. 23.

* The 88 bars of the score must be completed by a whole-bar rest, in accordance with the Bülow analyses of Beethoven.

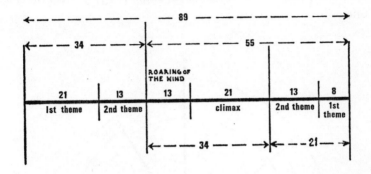

FIG. 23

The Fibonacci series reflects, in fact, the law of *natural growth*. To take a simple example. If every branch of a tree, in one year shoots a new branch, and these new branches are doubled after two years, the number of the branches shows the following yearly increase: 2, 3, 5, 8, 13, 21, 34 · · ·

"We follow nature in composition," wrote Bartók, and was indeed directed by *natural* phenomena to his discovery of these regularities. He was constantly augmenting his collection of plants, insects and mineral specimens. He called the sunflower his favourite plant, and was extremely happy whenever he found fir-cones placed on his desk. According to Bartók "also folk music is a phenomenon of nature. Its formations developed as spontaneously as other living natural organisms: the flowers, animals, etc." ("At the Sources of Folk Music": 1925).

This is why the form-world of Bartók's music reminds us most directly of *natural* pictures and formations.

The GS of a circle, having 360°, subtends an angle of 222·5° on one hand, and 137·5° on the other. It can be observed in a large number of plants, e.g. palms, poplars, catkins, etc., that each bud, twig or leaf subtends an angle of 137·5° with the next one.

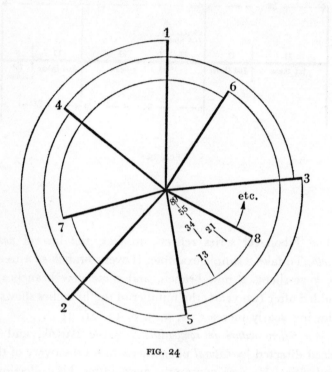

FIG. 24

Also, each new branch divides the *former* fields of section according to the rules of GS: so twig 3 divides the right-hand field between 1 and 2; twig 4 the left-hand field between 1 and 2; twig 5 does the same with the field between 2 and 3, *ad inf.**

* The Fibonacci series appears this time as well: field between 2 and 3 is divided by 5, between 3 and 5 by 8, between 5 and 8 by 13, etc.

30

If we consider the process of the fugue of *Music for Strings, Percussion and Celesta* (analysed on pages 27–8) as a circum-volution,* its structure will surprisingly correspond to Fig. 24.

Or let us examine the diagrammatic sketch of the chambered shell of the cepalophod nautilus—Jules Verne was so interested in this sea shell that he named his famous *Nautilus* after it.

The diagonals drawn in any direction through the centre provide a pattern in which the centre always remains in the positive or negative GS section of the fields marked A–B, B–C, C–D, D–E, E–F, F–G.

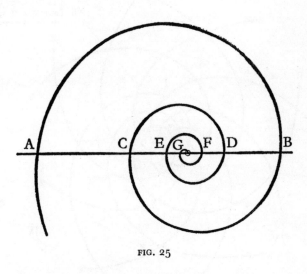

FIG. 25

This scheme is strikingly similar to the musical structures illustrated in Figs. 16 and 22.

---

* Also the theme moves round the circle of fifths—from the A centre back to the A centre.

But the most revealing example is presented by the structure of the *fir-cone*. Proceeding from the centre of its disc, logarithmic spirals are seen to move clockwise and anti-clockwise in a closed system where the numbers of the spirals *always* represent values of the Fibonacci series.

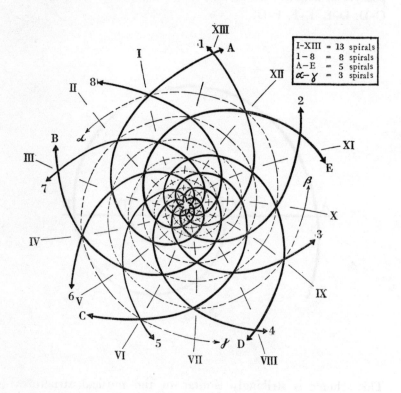

I–XIII	= 13 spirals
1 – 8	= 8 spirals
A – E	= 5 spirals
α – γ	= 3 spirals

FIG. 26a

(If we turn the cone upside down, we can also see the system of two spirals along the junction lines of the scales). Each of the spiral systems contain all the scales of the cone. There are cones in which the numbers of the spirals present still higher series values: 3, 5, 8, 13, 21.

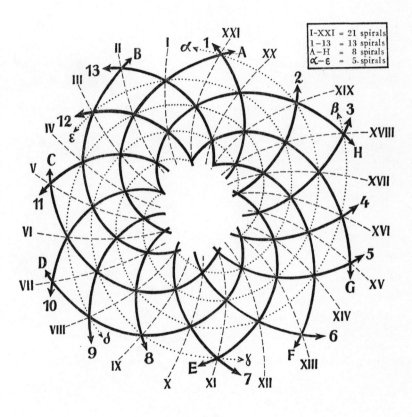

FIG. 26b

Similar arrangements can be observed in sunflowers, daisies, ananas, etc., also in the convolutions of the stems of leaves on numerous plants. Frequently the serial numbers 21, 34, 55, 89 and even 144 and 233 are encountered in these spiral systems.

For example, the sunflower has 34 petals and its spirals have the values of 21, 34, 55, 89, 144.

It is interesting to note that the GS is always associated only with *organic* matter and is quite foreign to the inorganic world.*

* The irrational number in the formula of GS precludes its occurrence in crystal-forms.

The Use of Chords and Intervals

Chromatic System

The study of these proportions leads us immediately to the question of Bartók's use of chords and intervals. His chromatic system is based on the laws of GS and especially, Fibonacci's numerical series.

Calculated in semi-tones:

2 stands for a major second,
3 ,, ,, minor third,
5 ,, ,, perfect fourth,
8 ,, ,, minor sixth,
13 ,, an augmented octave, etc.

For the present, the musical tissue may be imagined as built up exclusively of cells 2, 3, 5, 8, and 13 in size, with sub-divisions following the proportions provided by the above series. Thus, the 8 may be broken up only into 5 + 3. (The possibility of a division into 4 + 4 or 7 + 1 is precluded by the system.)

This cell division can be well observed in the finale of the *Divertimento*. The principal theme appears in the course of the movement in five variations: in Fig. 27 we have grouped them according to size, and indicated with each variation the characteristic division. The initial form of the theme is $3 + 2 = 5$.

FIG. 27

Since the fifth line (in Fig. 27) continues on the previous one, in its fourth bar the melody rises not by a minor third (3), as in the previous line, but by a perfect fourth (5), thus conforming to a GS augmentation.

Fig. 28 gives the successive themes in the first movement of the *Sonata for Two Pianos and Percussion*. The range of the leitmotif is 8 semi-tones, divided by the fundamental note C into $5 + 3$ semi-tones. The principal theme comprises 13 semi-tones divided by the fundamental note C into $5 + 8$. (See also Fig. 64.) The first phrase of the secondary theme extends

36

13 semi-tones, from G down to F♯; while the second phrase, 21 semi-tones from B down to D.

The melodies follow each other in GS order:

Leitmotif	$3 + 5 = 8$
Principal theme	$5 + 8 = 13$
Secondary theme	$13, 21$

FIG. 28

From the point of view of *harmonic* architecture, this exposition also bears witness to a systematic arrangement. The principal theme gets its magical tone-colour from a *pentatonic* harmony

(see Fig. 29a),* the formula of which is $2+3+2$. In the middle
of the principal theme there comes an ostinato built $3+5+3$,
Ab major-minor (see Fig. 29b): C–Eb–Ab–B, the fourth,
Eb–Ab, is further divided by an F♯ into $3+2$. Parallel fourths
(5) and minor sixths (8) join the secondary theme (see Fig. 29c).
This is seen clearly also in the recapitulation from b. 292.
Finally (see Fig. 29d) the closing theme is accompanied
throughout by parallel minor sixths (8).

FIG. 29

Thus each new harmony rises one step higher in the GS order,
i.e.

principal theme	$2+3+2$
middle part	$3+5+3$
secondary theme	$5+8$
closing theme	8

A similar correlation of motifs is encountered in the *Miraculous
Mandarin*:

* It appears also in the melody, bs. 37–39: Ab–F♯–Eb–Db and
F♯–E–C♯–B.

FIG. 30

It is interesting to note that in Bartók's music, in spite of the frequency of parallels, major third and major sixth parallels seldom occur, because such parallels cannot be fitted into the GS system, being quite incongruous to it. We could even speak of the *prohibition* of these parallels in the same sense that parallel fifths and octaves are forbidden in classical harmony. On the other hand we meet at every step with minor third (3), perfect fourth (5), minor sixth (8), and even major second (2) parallels.

The major third has no noteworthy *melodic* function either, the more natural, almost self-evident is the motivic role of the minor third:

FIG. 31

This is the reason why, whenever Bartók used a triad in a *chromatic* movement, he placed the minor third *over* the fundamental note and the major third *below* it, the chord thus acquiring the proportion 8:5:3.

FIG. 32a

From the synthesis of these two emerged the most typical Bartók chord, the well-known "major-minor" form, consisting of a minor third–perfect fourth–minor third $(3+5+3)$. This major-minor chord is often completed by the seventh of the root, e.g. an E–G–C–E♭ chord with a B♭ (see also Fig. 29b).

40

FIG. 32b

41

This major-minor chord has a number of synonym forms, to which we shall give (for want of a better term) the collective designation: type *alpha* (α), and we shall call the different sections of it by the letters *beta* (β), *gamma* (γ), *delta* (δ) and *epsilon* (ε). This type occurs as frequently in Bartók's music as do the seventh-chords in nineteenth-century music:

FIG. 33

These chords are exclusively built up of GS intervals (2, 3, 5, 8), as follows:

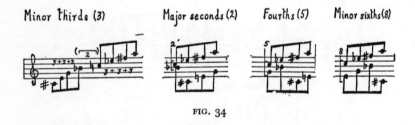

FIG. 34

and do not contain the characteristic intervals of the overtone system—fifth, major third and the minor seventh.*

* From here arises the characteristic "glow " of the alpha harmonies. Perhaps the most tense chord in Baroque music was the diminished seventh. This tension is increased in Bartók's *alpha* chords through the merging of two diminished seventh chords.

Type α can readily be reduced to the relations of the *axis system*. In order to feel the tonality of a chord, we need at least two notes: in the simplest case the root, say C, and its fifth G, or its major third E, when G or E respectively supports the C.* Let us put this relation in GS form:

FIG. 35

According to the axis system, the tone G (or E) may be replaced by any other of the corresponding axis (G–E–B♭–C♯) without changing the tonal character of C. We can therefore substitute E, B♭ or even C♯ for G.

FIG. 36a

The four intervals sounding together result in the chord *beta* (β). It should be noted that the combination of the first three intervals is no novelty to us, since it is identical with the chord of a major seventh: C–E–G–B♭.

---

* Tonality can only be established through the asymmetrical division of the tonal system; in case of equal division we would be unable to determine the root.

A similar axis substitution may be carried out with the note C without changing its function. We can thus replace C by E♭, F♯ or A, all belonging to the same axis.

FIG. 36b

In the form *delta* the first three intervals are summarised.

Chord *alpha* is therefore practically an axis-like application of the simple C–G, or C–E–G relation; the only stipulation being that the chord should be composed of *two layers* ("axes"): that of the tonic and the corresponding dominant.*

FIG. 37

* The two layers (T and D) correspond to the root and overtone relation of classical harmony. It is pertinent that also in traditional music, functional attractions were based on these two layers. The authentic (cadential) connected chords require that the root of the first chord becomes an *overtone* of the chord following. (Classical harmony calls these common notes.) Thus, in the progression T to S, the root of I (C) becomes a fifth in IV, or a seventh in II. Connecting S and D the root of II (D) or IV (F) becomes fifth or seventh in V. Connecting D and T the root of V (G) becomes fifth in I.

45

FIG. 38

Type *epsilon* (ϵ) is seldom used since its tonal character is unstable, due to the absence of G without which the root does not receive sufficient support.

Certain sections of the *alpha* chord have been familiar to us from classical harmony: E–G–B♭–C is the C major seventh, G–B♭–C–E♭ is the C minor seventh, B♭–C–E♭–F♯ (G♭) is the C seventh chord based on a diminished triad. Novelty is produced by the introduction of the relative A, and primarily by the C♯. In fact the chord *beta* is an inversion of the ninth chord: C–E–G–B♭–D♭ (C♯) to C♯–E–G–B♭–C.

46

Essentially, type *alpha* is an axis harmony. As an example let us take the simplest case. If the C major and its relative A minor are replaced by C *minor* and A *major*,

FIG. 39

and these two chords are combined, then *beta, gamma* and *delta* will be equally readable in the resulting harmonies. This chord bears a high counterpole tension due to the diverse tonal character of its components, expressed by the difference of six accidentals—the three flat signs of the C minor and the three sharp signs of the A major.

In accordance with the stratification of the *alpha* type it is possible to build up a still more extended *alpha* pile:

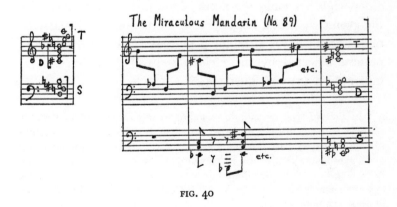

FIG. 40

From a succession of diminished triads a "closed" sequence is derived since, by the periodic repetition of the intervals we are taken back to the starting point:

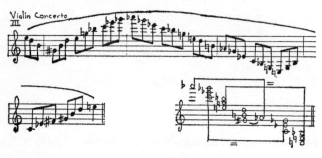

FIG. 41

And now we come to the very gist! That GS is not an external restriction but one of the most intrinsic laws of music is demonstrated by *pentatony*—perhaps the most ancient human sound system—which may be regarded as a pure musical expression of the GS principle. In the *la-so-mi* figures of the oldest children songs the notes of the melody are tuned after the geometric mean, i.e. after GS. Pentatony, particularly the most ancient forms of minor pentatony (*la* and *re*), rests on a pattern reflected by the melody steps of major second (2), minor third (3) and fourth (5).*

* In the old-type pentatonic melodies with a changing-fifth structure (usually *la-so-mi + re-do-la* or *la-so-mi-re + re-do-la-so* scale) the major third plays a secondary part. To quote Kodály: "It is clear that the pentatony and the fifth construction are independent, more so, stylistically opposite." According to Kodály the falling minor third, *so-mi*, rather than *do-re-mi* or any other simple configuration is what the child seems first to feel as a basic musical relationship—representing the earliest musical expression of a human being.

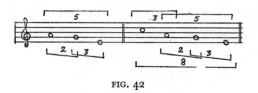

FIG. 42

This aspect of GS architecture is markedly evident in the *Dance Suite* which appropriately has been called the "Eastern European Symphony". The make-up of the GS system can here be followed step by step, for this work—a rich and complex musical universe based on the primordial elements of pentatony —reveals the evolution of this technique.

The first movement arises from major seconds (2); the second is built on minor thirds (3); the third summarises these former elements $(2 + 3 + 2 + 3 + 2)$, presenting a pure pentatonic scale. The harmonies of this movement are based on $5 + 5$. Finally, the melody of the fourth movement follows the pattern $8 = 5 + 3$, where $5 = 3 + 2$.

FIG. 43

49

Type *alpha* can also be derived from *pentatony*. This is how Bartók transforms a pentatonic scale into *beta* and *gamma* structures:

FIG. 44

This type of harmonies originating from folk song was suggested by Bartók himself in "The Folk Songs of Hungary" (Pro Musica: 1928):*

FIG. 45

---

* At first it may seem astonishing that in Bartók's music pentatony is so closely allied to chromaticism. But this relation is natural, as with Bartók the primordial attractions of pentatony carry *tension*, and just this tension finds adequate forms of expression in his GS system.

50

We now mention a frequently recurring group of GS-type chords which structurally represent intervals of 1:5, 1:3 and 1:2. The GS relation between these three formulae results from the proportion 5:3:2. Each of these arise from the periodic repetition of intervals 1:5, 1:3, or 1:2 respectively. Their structure is, consequently, as follows:

Model 1:5 alternating minor seconds and perfect fourths
e.g. C–C♯–F♯–G–C . . .

Model 1:3 alternating minor seconds and minor thirds
e.g. C–C♯–E–F–G♯–A–C . . .

Model 1:2 alternating minor and major seconds
e.g. C–C♯–E♭–E–F♯–G–A–B♭–C . . .

and hereby, they form clearly *closed* systems.*

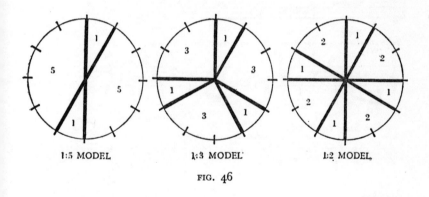

1:5 MODEL   1:3 MODEL   1:2 MODEL

FIG. 46

* The influence of folk music is possibly also responsible for Model 1:5, e.g. Movement III of *Suite op. 14* was inspired by Arab folk music. Perfect examples of 1:2 and 1:3 models have been found in compositions of Liszt and Rimsky-Korsakov.

FIG. 46a

FIG. 46c

We attribute the greatest importance to Model 1:2 since it actually represents a scale-group of the *axis* shown in Fig. 47, i.e. C–C♯–E♭–E–F♯–G–A–B♭.

FIG. 47

It can also be called the "basic scale" of Bartók's chromatic system, with whose help the tonality of even his most complicated chromatic melodies and chords can be determined. And here we arrive at an important discovery.

There exists an organic correlation between the *axis* system, the *alpha* chords and Models 1:2 and 1:5. If we detach the upper C–A–F♯–E♭ and the lower G–E–C♯–B♭ layers of the axis (see the centre part of Fig. 48) and pile up one on the other, we obtain the *alpha* chord (see top left of Fig. 48). If we separate the pole-counterpole relations (C–F♯ and A–E♭, respectively) of the axis, we have Model 1:5 (see right bottom of Fig. 48). If we combine the notes of the axis we get a Model 1:2 (see top right of Fig. 48).

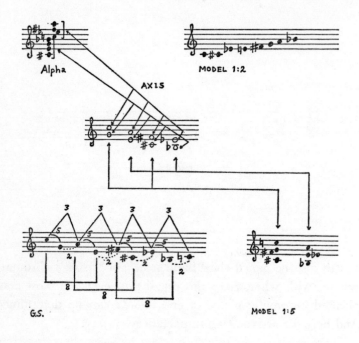

FIG. 48

In respect to tonality these formulae are inseparable. The fundamental role of the 1:2 model is only emphasised by the inclusion of all the potentialities of the tonic (C–E♭–F♯–A) major, minor, seventh, and alpha chords, as well as Models 1:5.

FIG. 49

These formulae merge into each other so that it is sometimes rather difficult to define where one of them ends and the other begins.*

FIG. 50

* The tonal resting point in Model 1:2 always falls on the *lower* note of the minor second, which is the upper note of the major second. In the case of Model 1:2 on C tonic, it is C, or E♭, or F♯ or A. Thus the base note of the minor second, major third, fifth and minor seventh is always the lower note, while that of the major second, fourth, minor sixth and major seventh, is the upper note. In the case of the minor third, tritone or major sixth, any of the notes may serve as base, as they all lie on the same axis.

57

And this is the reason why the most characteristic axis melodies in Bartók are exclusively ruled by GS principles (see bottom left of Fig. 48).

FIG. 51

Within the range of the twelve-tone scale three different 1:2 models can be constructed:

> a *tonic*, C–C♯–E♭–E–F♯–G–A–B♭;
> a *dominant*, C♯–D–E–F–G–A♭–B♭–B; and
> a *subdominant*, D–E♭–F–F♯–A♭–A–B–C.

Every other form agrees with one or other of the above formulae.

I would like to illustrate the interrelations outlined above, by three brief examples. The *Notturno* in *Mikrokosmos* follows the tonic–tonic–dominant–tonic structure of the new-type Hungarian folk songs. So its first, second, and fourth lines fulfil tonic functions, accentuated by the tune which constitutes a *tonic Model 1:2.*

FIG. 52

Its tonal character is determined by the A-fourth step (E–A), completed by the harmonies into a complete tonic axis:

FIG. 53

The piece called *From the Island of Bali* (Mikrokosmos No. 109) rests on the G♯–B–D–F axis. Its scale provides a full Model 1:2 (G♯–A–B–C–D–E♭–F–G♭) which, as apparent from the final chords can be considered as a *B-fifth** (B–G♭=B–F♯) and *G♯-fifth* (G♯–E♭=A♭–E♭), and as a *F-fourth* (C–F) and *D-fourth* (A–D), covering the complete axis.

FIG. 54

Both right and left hands play separate 1:5 models (G♯–A–D–E♭ and B–C–F–G♭)** and these are characterised by their counter-pole relations: left hand, G♯-fifth+D-fourth, right hand, B-fifth+F-fourth.

Also the formal construction of the piece is adjusted to the

---

* Here we mention the problem of *enharmonic* alteration. "It is highly desirable that we have a system of notation of twelve equivalent symbols," writes Bartók, adding that he was always guided by questions of readability when writing his scores. That is the reason why we frequently find the enharmonic variants in the piano reductions of his orchestral works. Our method of notation "originates in the diatonic system and therefore it is an utterly useless tool when it comes to recording twelve-tone music"—Bartók: *The Problem of Modern Music* (1920).

** Thus by the merging of two Models 1:5 we obtain Model 1:2.

F–B–G♯–D axis. The first section closes in F, ending at the double-bar. The middle first moves around B, then G♯, with an extended D pedal-point at the second double-bar. The final chord is a synthesis of D major and F minor, and may be considered at the same time as type *alpha* (F♯–A–C–D–F–A♭).

FIG. 55

Our third example is the recapitulation theme of the *Violin Concerto*, representing axis E–G–A♯–C♯. Its scale is of Model 1:2 (E–F–G–G♯–A♯–B–C♯–D). Bars 1 and 2 are based on the C♯, E (melody) and G (harmony) poles of the axis. Bar 6 circumscribes the E-gamma chord (E major–minor, G♯–B–E–G), and the melody of bars 5–13, the 1:5 model (B–E–F–A♯).

FIG. 56

We have to mention also a third type of chromatic chord—namely the chords of *equal intervals*. Its most frequent forms in the GS system are the whole-tone scale, chord of diminished seventh, chord in fourths and the augmented triad. The last has its justification in Bartók's chromaticism only in so far as it is built of minor sixths (8+8+8).

Whole-tone scale	2+2+2+2+2+2
Diminished seventh	3+3+3+3
Chord in fourths	5+5+5+5 · · ·
Augmented triad	8+8+8

In our tone system two whole-tone scales can be distinguished: they are "geometrical dominants", complementary patterns of each other: C–D–E–F#–G#–A# and C#–Eb–F–G–A–B.

FIG. 57

Bartók liked to use whole-tone chords *before climaxes*, since it has the effect, as it were, of "melting" the sounds (see Fig. 57: *Bluebeard's Castle* No. 136, *The Wooden Prince* No. 123, *Music* Mov. I b. 48, Mov. II b. 56, Mov. III b. 14).

Harmonisation and theme construction in *fourth chords* are strikingly frequent, due to the influence of Hungarian peasant music.

FIG. 58

Chords in fourths generally allow two combinations: one according to the 2:3 *pentatonic* principle, the other after the 1:5 model.

(a) Of the two fourth chords in the 2:3 scale we can treat the one, which lies a major second (2) higher or a minor third (3) lower than the other, as *tonic*, and this can be reduced to the *do-so→la* cadence of the older folk songs:

FIG. 59

(b) A good example of 1:5 association is the closing theme in Movement II of the *Music for Strings, Percussion and Celesta*. The 1:5 models are based on two fourth chords: D–G–C–F and A♭–D♭–G♭–C♭–F♭.

64

1:5
models
$\left\{\begin{array}{l} A\flat–D\flat–D–G \\ D\flat–G\flat–G–C \\ G\flat–C\flat–C–F \end{array}\right.$

FIG. 60

The GS chords and chords of equal intervals often combine together, in practice. Fig. 61 shows an ostinato from Mov. I of the *Sonata for Two Pianos and Percussion*. The twelve tones of the ostinato contain the entire chromatic scale.

FIG. 61

The upper part is based on the A–B–D♭–E♭–F–G whole-tone scale, and the lower on the complementary F♯–G♯–B♭–C–D–E whole-tone scale. Each part is composed of minor sixths; the upper of A–F–D♭ and B–G–E♭ augmented triads, and the lower of F♯–D–B♭ and G♯–E–C augmented triads $(8+8+8)$. The two parts move in parallel minor thirds (3). The ostinato is characterised by the 1:3 models and the *gamma* harmonies $(3+5+3)$.

65

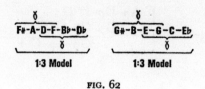

FIG. 62

The beginning and final notes assume a pole-counterpole relationship: in the upper part, A and E♭, and in the lower, F♯ and C. When viewed together they form an axial arrangement, F♯–A–C–E♭. Every component of the structure is of GS formula.

Diatonic System

Bartók's diatony is simply an exact and systematic *inversion* of the laws of his chromatic technique, i.e. the GS rules.

1. The most characteristic form of Bartók's "diatonic" system is the *acoustic* (overtone) scale, C–D–E–F♯–G–A–B♭–C, and the *acoustic* chord (major triad with minor seventh and augmented fourth, e.g. C major with B♭ and F♯). It is called acoustic because its tones derive from the natural overtone series.

The Wooden Prince

ppp

Contrasts, Vln., Clar., Pft.

Cantata Profana

"Spring" - No. 16 of 27 Choruses

Duke Bluebeard's Castle Op. 11

"dearest Bluebeard"

FIG. 63

In the finale of the *Sonata for Two Pianos and Percussion*, for example, the acoustic scale C–D–E–F♯–G–A–B♭ enfolds itself above the C–E–G (C major) chord: see Fig. 64. This scale is dominated by the major third, perfect fifth, "natural seventh", and further by the augmented (acoustic) fourth and the major sixth (with Bartók, the "pastoral sixth"). All this in contrast to the minor third, perfect fourth, minor sixth (3:5:8, C–E♭–F–A♭) milieu of the GS system.

Let us place the principal themes of the chromatic First Movement and the diatonic Third Movement, side by side. The "chromatic" theme is composed of GS cells, the melodic line hinges on minor third, perfect fourth, minor sixth intervals (3–5–8). The "diatonic" theme is a perfect acoustic scale.

FIG. 64

These two spheres of harmony complement each other to such measure that the chromatic scale can be separated into a GS sequence and an acoustic scale.*

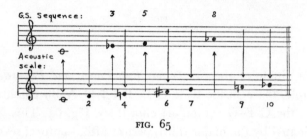

FIG. 65

In the acoustic scale the major third replaces the minor third (3), the augmented fourth replaces the perfect fourth (5), and the major sixth replaces the minor sixth (8).

Incidentally, let me refer here to the *la-so-mi* figures in the oldest childrens' songs and primitive folk music, which, by no stretch of imagination can be regarded as products of some deliberate planning, though the notes accord with the "geometric mean", i.e. GS. Likewise, when listening to traditional music, it seldom occurs to us that the consonance of a simple *major triad* might result from the coincidence of the nearest natural overtones: our ears simply register the fundamental number relations in the vibrations of the perfect fifth and major third.

In Movement I of the *Sonata for Two Pianos and Percussion*, the melodic and harmonic devises are derived from the most primitive *pentatonic* elements, while the principal theme in the Finale simply evolves the natural overtone scale over the C *major* chord (see Fig. 64). Yet this major triad comes as a revelation. How can a simple major chord produce such an explosive effect?

Looked at from another angle, may a composer with a

* The C♯ and B, as chromatic intervals, require a chromatic interpretation.

70

pretence of being up-to-date avail himself at all of the major triad, whose vital significance has long so worn off and became an empty husk? Actually, the *elemental* effect of Bartók's music is due, for the most part, to his method of reducing expression to simple and primary symbols. The major triad may in itself be a hollow cliché, but when brought into a *polar-dual* relationship with another system—as done by Bartók—it may regain its original and potent significance.

The explanation is that the GS between two points always cuts into the *most tense* point, whereas symmetry creates *balance*. The overtone series is devoid of tension because its notes are integer multiples of the fundamental note's vibrations.* The thrilling effect of the major triad in the Finale of the Sonata is a direct result of it being completely released from the constraints of the GS system.

So the *la-so-mi* (pentatony) and the *major triad* are not only symbols of the purest music but also elements of structure and formation, which, in Bartók's interrelation regain the fire only they may once have possessed. This is what I would like to denote as the elemental rebirth of music through the reconstruction of its means.

Let us set up the formula of the work:

DYNAMIC proportion = GS–forms = pentatony = opening movement

STATIC proportion = symmetry = overtones = closing movement

* The GS expresses the law of the *geometric* mean, the overtones reflect the law of the *arithmetic* mean. As we know, harmonic overtones are produced by the vibration of strings, air in tubes, etc.; these not only vibrate to their full length but also in halves, thirds, fourths, etc. of the length—producing *symmetrical* nodes on the string or in the tube. The overtones combine with the basic note, and the *colour* of the tone is determined by the extent to which these overtones modify the sound. We therefore call the harmonies of the acoustic system "colour chords". It is no accident that the acoustic effects in Bartók's compositions originate primarily in the colour chords of French impressionism. Bartók himself used to allude to this inspiration.

This implies that the symmetrical periodisation of the Viennese classical school and its harmonic system of overtone relations are phenomena not independent of each other; they only represent different (horizontal-vertical) projections of the same basic concept.

2. The two systems reflect each other in an *inverse* relationship. Through the inversion of GS intervals, acoustic intervals are obtained—from a major second (2) a natural seventh (e.g. from B♭–C, C–B♭), from a minor third (3) a major sixth, from a perfect fourth (5) a fifth, from a minor sixth (8) a major third—the most characteristic acoustic intervals. Therefore not only do they complement, but also *reflect* each other organically.

The opening and closing of the *Cantata Profana* offers a beautiful illustration, two scales mirroring each other note for note—a GS scale (intervals 2, 3, 5, 8 with a diminished fifth) and a pure acoustic scale:

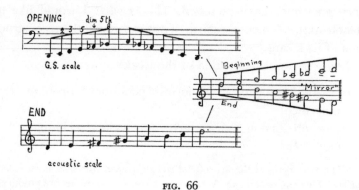

FIG. 66

It is worth clarifying this interrelation from another point of view. The harmony which appears beneath the *acoustic* melody of Fig. 64 produces perhaps the greatest surprise of the work, obtained by means of a simple major chord: C–E–G.

72

FIG. 67a

This consists of the closest *overtone* relations, i.e. a perfect fifth and major third. In the chromatic First Movement the major triad always emerges in the $3 + 5 = 8$ division of the GS:

FIG. 67b

The characteristic perfect fourth (5) and minor sixth (8) of this GS chord have been transformed by *inversion* into the *perfect fifth* and *major third* of the acoustic chord respectively.

Let us show these chords in their seventh forms too:

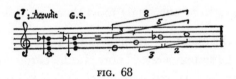

FIG. 68

What is valid, relative to the C root, in the GS system from above *downwards* is equally valid in the acoustic system in the *opposite* direction. It is therefore an "overtone" chord. The circumstance that our ancient melodies have a *descending* character may perhaps be related to the fact that pentatony is a GS tone-sequence.

3. Although these features seem to appertain to the outward form, this no longer applies when it is considered that only *consonant* intervals exist in the acoustic system (owing to overtone

consonance) whereas the GS avails itself precisely of those intervals which have been considered *dissonant* by musical theory from the time of Palestrina. Incidentally, this diversity accounts for the tendency of Western music to be acoustic and of Eastern to be pentatonic.

This implies that the relation of consonance and dissonance is also inverted in the two harmony-worlds; the purity of a diatonic consonance is in direct proportion to the overtones, while the chromatic technique attains its highest degree of consonance when all the twelve semi-tones in the tempered scale are made to sound together—"like the roar of the sea", to quote Bartók.

4. A secret of Bartók's music, and perhaps the most profound, is that the "closed" world of the GS is counterbalanced by the "open" sphere of the acoustic system. The former always pre-supposes the presence of the *complete* system—it is not accidental that we have always depicted chromatic formations in the *closed* circle of fifths. (See Figs. 2, 4, 46, 48.) In the last, all relations are dependent on *one* tone since the natural sequence of over-tones emerges from one single root: therefore it is *open*.

5. Thus, the diatonic system has a fundamental, *root* note and the chromatic system a *central* note. In the chromatic system all relations can be inverted without changing the significance of the central note. The principal theme of the recapitulation in the *Violin Concerto* has a B tonality, in spite of the fact that the B major tonic "stands on its head" (owing to the inversion of the theme) and our ears, accustomed only to overtone relations, perceive it as having an "E minor" tonality. (The B centre is accentuated by a shimmering pedal-point too):

FIG. 69

It is this "mirror" (see Fig. 69) which shows that the chromatic technique leaves the requirements of the overtone system out of consideration, and ideas like "up" and "down" become quite meaningless in it. The harmony which in the preceding example sounds below the B centre, produces, by the negation of the overtone system, an effect as if the objects of the physical world have suddenly become weightless—a sphere where the laws of gravity are no longer valid (see Mov. I, b. 194).

6. And this is why Bartók's GS system always involves the concentric *expansion* or *contraction* of intervals which is as consistent as to be virtually inseparable from the chromatic technique.

For example, the quoted themes from the First Movement of the *Sonata for Two Pianos and Percussion* are constructed in ever-widening orbits (see Fig. 28: leitmotif–principal theme– secondary theme 8–13–21). The principal theme is augmented from bar to bar, from minor third to fourth, sixth and seventh intervals. And the scope of the secondary theme expands similarly step by step, first with pentatonic turns, then with fourth and fifth intervals, finally resolving in a broad sixth (see Fig. 28).

We frequently find a "funnel-shaped" (see Fig. 90) and "scissor-like" movement of notes,

FIG. 70

and sequences proceeding by wider and wider steps:

75

FIG. 71

Even these processes follow a planned course, every detail showing augmentation up to the geometric centre of the movement (b. 217), after which they gradually contract again.

On the other hand, in the diatonic Third Movement, such progressions are quite *unimaginable*. The diatonic harmonies are characterised by a *static* firmness (e.g. the chord of Fig. 67a radiates its energy for a long period of time with a motionless, unwavering constancy) in contrast to the GS system, which is always of a *dynamic* character.

7. Bartók's *closed* (chromatic) world may well be symbolised by the circle, while his *open* (diatonic) system, by the straight line. Like in *Dante's* Divine Comedy the symbol of the Inferno is the circle, the ring, while that of the Paradiso, the straight line, the arrow, the ray. The rings of the Inferno undergo a concentric diminution till they arrive at the "Cocitus", whereas those of the Paradiso widen into the infinite "Empyreum".

In Bartók's "cosmos" the themes follow a similar pattern; chromaticism is most naturally associated with the "circular" while diatony with the "straight line" of melody: see Fig. 72.

8. The idea of "open" and "closed" is also expressed by the organisation of the themes in relation to *time*. The basis of

76

FIG. 72

a classical melody is the *period*. As a rule, the themes in the music of Haydn, Mozart and Beethoven are divided into 8 + 8, 4 + 4 and 2 + 2 bars: the first two-bar "question" being followed by a two-bar "answer"; these four bars may then be considered as a single question, the answer to which being given in bars 5–8. Thus the form developes: this simple 8-bar sentence ends in a half-close and corresponds to the tonic, full-close ending of the 16-bar period. This principle of symmetrical periodisation is readily discerned in Bartók's diatonic mode of writing as well.

In contrast to this, in his GS technique, positive and negative sections constitute quite a different system of "questions" and "answers" (see Figs. 16 and 22). Here the law of balance and symmetrical periodisation is replaced by regularities of *tense asymmetry*. Positive and negative sections embrace each other like the ascending and descending parts of a wave.

The conditions of organisation in the GS system are inversely related to those in the symmetrical periodisation: one provides for a process of *merging*, the other for *dividing* its constituents; the former emphasises the *organic unity* in time, the latter surveys the material in space. The GS forms assume the character of an uninterrupted time process, revolving in the arc of a wave, while the symmetrical periodisation breaks the material into metrical components of lines, rhymes and strophes, as in the construction of a verse.

9. And what do the two systems look like when examined in number relations? The key-numbers of the overtone system are *whole* numbers: those of the octave—2, 4, 8; of the fifth—3, 6, 12; of the major third—5, 10, etc. While in the GS system the key number is *irrational*:

$$\frac{\sqrt{5}-1}{2} = 0.6180340\ldots$$

The irrational character becomes still more explicit if the formula is written as follows (which again conceals the Fibonacci series):

$$\frac{5}{8}\left\{\frac{3}{5}\left\{\frac{2}{3}\left\{\cfrac{1}{1+\cfrac{1}{\ldots 1+\cfrac{1}{\ldots\ldots 1+\cfrac{1}{\ldots\ldots\ldots\ldots 1+1}}}}\right.\right.\right. \ldots \text{ad inf.} = 0.618\ldots$$

The acoustic system rests on *arithmetical*, the GS system on *geometrical* proportions. (See App. III.) The characteristic 3–5–8 proportion is only approximately correct and is expressible only in irrational numbers (e.g. 5:8.09061 . . .). The minor third in pentatony can be proved to be somewhat larger than it is in the tempered system.*

10. It may be symbolic that in the diatonic system the partial-tones range *above* while in the chromatic system *below* the fundamental note (see Fig. 68). It is of some interest that Riemann derives the minor triads from "under"-tones and the major triads from "over"-tones.

In the case of GS *alpha* chords this relation is also valid, inversely; the minor third falls above and the major third below the key-note. Although Riemann's concept may be

* The order-number of the minor third in the tempered system is 1:19 and in the pentatonic system, 1:21. (The thirds of the so-called Transdanubian pentatony come close to the major third.)

contestable it is still worth considering the fact that the *two most intense* GS intervals produceable within the compass of an octave are identical with the chord Riemann produced by inverting and projecting the major triad in the lower range (C–A♭–F): $8 = $ C–A♭, $5 = $ C–F.

The leitmotif of the *Miraculous Mandarin** receives its intensity from just these GS intervals: A♭–F = G♯–F. (See Fig. 31.)

* In the score of the *Miraculous Mandarin* each person is represented by a tone-symbol with whose aid we may well "read" the plot of the pantomime. The Mandarin may be recognised from the notes G♯–F (A♭–F); the Girl from the notes E♭–B♭ or E♭–B♭–E (D♯–A♯ or D♯–A♯–E)—see the very beginning of the work. The fact that the compliments of the Old Gallant are intended for the Girl is shown also by the music: the basic chord of the Old Gallant, more than thirty times, leads to the Girl's symbol:

We mention only three brief examples. After the entry of the Mandarin the pentatonic ostinato undulates from the Mandarin's G♯–F notes to the Girl's tone-symbol:

or later when he is trying to reach the Girl:

We see the *union* of the two symbols at the very end of the work:

A detailed analysis of the pantomime was published by the author in *Studia Musicologica* (Vol. 1 No. 2, pp. 363–432, in German).

A particularly effective application of these inverted relations can be observed at the climax, in the C-major scene of *Bluebeard's Castle*, when the stage is plunged into darkness:

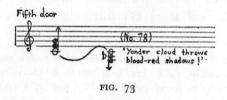

FIG. 73

11. Further food for thought is that in Bartók's music the motif-line generally attains its most tense point on the minor sixth (or perfect fourth) of the tonic. The climax of the sixth is basically a property of classical music where it functions as the *subdominant*.

FIG. 74

It is known that the most intense harmonic function in classical music is represented by the subdominant, but it comes as a surprise that the *minor subdominant*, being the intensest of all subdominant chords, is essentially a characteristic form of GS tension:

FIG. 75

This means nothing less than that the technique of tension-relaxation in classical music is closely related to the dual principle of GS and acoustic correlations: subdominant tension is, in fact, a *GS tension*, while dominant-tonic presents an *overtone* relationship.

Bartók's diatonic system results in *authentic*, while his chromatic system in *plagal*, harmonic interconnections; the basic step of the former being T–D–T and that of the latter, T–S–T (see Figs. 99–100 and App. II).

The S–T turn in the GS system can be reduced to the *re-la* close so frequently found in ancient pentatonic melodies. Compare with the changing-fifth and with the six-four types of old Hungarian peasant songs:

FIG. 76

12. Bartók's diatonic music is always inspired by an optimism and serenity, his chromatic music by a dark, moreover, irrational and demoniac passion. This involuntarily brings to mind the chromatic experiments of Liszt and Moussorgsky, probing the gloomy depths of life. Let us recall the late piano pieces of Liszt: *Grey Clouds, Unlucky Stars, Preludio Funebre,* the death-music *R. Wagner, Venezia,* the ghostly *Lugubre Gondola,* all these are written in a tone-system of distance models. Or the scene of *Boris Godunov's* frenzy, where Moussorgsky avails himself of a perfect "axis system".

All in all, the chromatic and diatonic systems form a coherent *whole,* representing two sides of the same coin, one of which negates and at the same time complements, the other. They constitute contrast in unity: affirm and deny, presuppose and exclude each other.*

* The same duality appears in the frequent use of the *complementary* keys. Two triads which merge *symmetrically* dissolve each other because the equidistance creates a floating tonality, so annihilates it. The programme of the *First String Quartet*—"illness" and "recovery"—is based on the duality of F minor and A major. These two triads complement each other, meeting in a closed distance model (1:3 model): F–A♭–C+A–C♯–E=F–A♭–A–C–C♯–E.

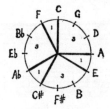

F minor + A major

In the piano piece "See-saw, dickory-daw" the floating is expressed by the combination of E minor and A♭ major (E–G–B+A♭–C–E♭ gives

In some of his works Bartók goes so far in the polarisation and reduction of his material, that form and content, means and meaning, seem to constitute an almost inseparable entity.

From the preceding principles every further *diatonic* formation becomes self-evident. The main diatonic intervals, i.e. the *fifth* and *major third*, are emphasised by the major chord, built up in successive thirds, every second degree of which rhymes in perfect fifths:

FIG. 77

a 1:3 model). Similarly the neutral *Klang* of E minor and A♭ major paints the hovering in the *Second Burlesque*: "A bit drunk" (see Fig. 46b). In *Bluebeard's Castle* the E major climax of the fifth door is destroyed by C minor at the entry of the blood-motif. Also, the tonal plan of the opera is built up of these enter-relations. The night is represented by F♯ minor, the daylight by its counterpole C major. C major may be neutralized by A♭ minor, thus the latter bears a "death"-symbolism in the work, while the complementary key of F♯ minor—B♭ major—is associated with the "love" scenes. These four triads include every degree of the twelve-note scale:

C–E–G	F♯–A–C♯
A♭–C♭–E♭	B♭–D–F

83

Here we have the origin of the well-known Bartók "signature".*

FIG. 78

(Cf. Two Portraits, Swiss Violin Concerto, Bagatelles Nos. 13 and 14, Ten easy piano pieces: "Dedication" and "Dawn", Mikrokosmos No. 70, etc.).

This type, combined with the acoustic fourth (e.g. C major chord with B and F♯), appears at the most splendid moments, as in the flower-garden of Bluebeard's Castle, or as the symbol of the "flaming, golden-haired noon": Fig. 79.

* This chord has a counterpart: the minor chord with major seventh, e.g. D–F–A–C♯, which is always associated with pain and passion in Bartók's dramatic works and songs ("Your leitmotif" wrote Bartók to Stefi Geyer). We give three brief examples from *Bluebeard's Castle*:

The *inversion* of this chord also plays a significant role; it has a baleful effect and signifies the ceasing of passion, death: "Eros turns downwards his torch!" At the end of *Bluebeard's Castle* we hear the chord C♯–F–A–C, the inversion of the tonic leitmotif C–E♭–G–B. By the inversion the tense C–E♭–G minor chord is transformed into the C–A–F major chord, based on the augmented triad C♯–F–A: from here the disorganising effect arises.

84

FIG. 79

Since the acoustic system is merely an inversion of the GS, we can obtain diatonic harmonies by *reversing* the layers of the *alpha* chord:

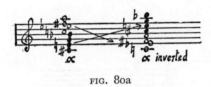

FIG. 80a

The diatonic effect is due to the alpha-inversion being governed by perfect fifths and major thirds (which were excluded by the *alpha* chords):

FIG. 80b

However paradoxical it may seem, the chord which has a major third above the key-note and a minor third below it, makes the most "diatonic", most opened impression in Bartók's music:

FIG. 81

And to complete the concatenation, it should be pointed out that the *inversion* of *alpha* contains the very kernel of the acoustic chord:

FIG. 82

It happens frequently that an ambiguous bass is sometimes represented by C and sometimes by F♯:

FIG. 83

This is the case in the "axis melody" of the theme in Movement III of *Music for Strings, Percussion and Celesta*:

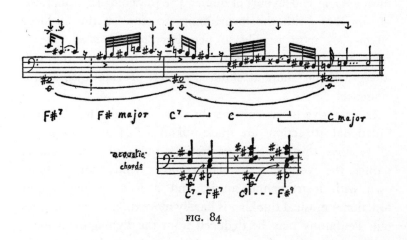

FIG. 84

We may summarise these analyses as follows:

GS TYPES (chromatic system)	ACOUSTIC TYPES (diatonic system)
Pentatony	Overtone chord and scale
Alpha chord	Inversion of alpha
1:2, 1:3, 1:5 models . .	Succession of thirds and fifths with major characteristics

Forms of equal intervals:. .
  whole-tone scale
  diminished seventh
  chord in fourths
  augmented triad, consisting
    of minor sixths
	Forms of equal intervals:
	  chord in fifths
	  augmented triad, consisting of major thirds

Particular significance may be attributed to the fact that *pentatony* is most characteristic of Bartók's chromatic (GS) system while *overtone* chords prevail in his diatonic system. This duality, in our opinion, would seem to express the two most ancient endeavours of music. The physiological apparatus of our ears (with the logarithmic structure of the cochlea) enables us most readily to perceive the *so-la-so-mi* (2:3:5) relations at the earliest stage, of which both primitive folk music and our simplest children's songs provide unequivocal evidence.

In primitive music-cultures the sense for major tonality and functional attractions are quite unknown.* The development of *harmonic* thinking derives from a quite different source, namely the overtone series. This could only have come into its own with instrumental music, and it is no accident that functional musical thinking is hardly more than a few centuries old. Pentatony may be deduced from the Pythagorean tonal system—grouping the nearest fifths and fourths—harmonic music from the overtone series.

Incidentally, pentatony is of *melodic*, linear origin, being of "horizontal" extent (in time) while the overtone system is of *harmonic* origin and has a "vertical" (spatial) dimension.

Would it be too daring to suppose that the roots of pentatonic and acoustic thinking were the two points of origin of all music.** (If so, then Bartók has penetrated to its inmost core.)

---

* "Pentatony does not suffer the dominant-tonic cadence." (Bartók: Hungarian Folk Music, 1933). "In this scale the fifth has no prevailing role" (Bartók: Hungarian Folk Music and New Hungarian Music, 1928). On the other hand "the frequent use of the fourth intervals in our melodies suggested to us the use of fourth-chords" (Bartók: The influence of peasant music on modern music, 1920).

** Bartók himself strongly believed that "it will be possible to trace back all the folk music on the face of the globe essentially to a few parent-forms, archetypes, ancient styles" (Bartók: Folk-song research and nationalism, 1937).

The first is justified by "inner" hearing, based on the *physio-logical* structure of the ear; the second by "external" hearing, controlled by the *physical* laws of consonance. The former is, therefore tense, expressive and *emotionally* charged, the latter colourful, impressive and *sensuous*.

The above claim is supported by the scientific observation that GS is to be met with in *organic* matter only. Pentatony, with all its tension, could neither have come into being without the aid of human emotion. The acoustic harmony on the other hand, may develop independently of the phenomenon of human life or of human intervention—a vibrating column of air in a pipe (or a string) is enough to bring it about.

Pentatonic and acoustic trends follow contradictory courses, Physiological efforts tend to *organise* and create *tension*, while physical efforts disorganise by striving to abolish tension. Here the thesis may be advanced that the GS creates a *closed* world and carries an inner tension, while the acoustic system is *open* and strives to release tension through its overtone consonances.

It may be added that this closedness is an organic feature of GS (see Figs. 24, 25 and 26 for examples independent of Bartók's tone-system) and this quality is responsible for the capacity of GS to *organise*. As an illustration: GS can be easily brought about if we bind a simple "knot" with a paper ribbon; without exception, every proportion of this knot will display geometric golden section.* Fig. 85.

* It is no accident that pentagons, so common in living nature, are foreign to the inorganic world.

$$d:c = c:b = b:a = 1:0\text{·}618$$

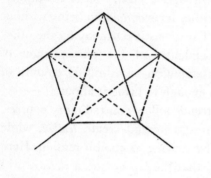
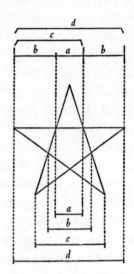

FIG. 85

It is this property of the pentagram that *Goethe* alludes to in Faust, Part I:

MEPH.: Let me admit; a tiny obstacle
        Forbids my walking out of here:
        It is the druid's foot upon your threshold.
FAUST: The *pentagram* distresses you?
        But tell me, then, you son of hell,
        If this impedes you, how did you come in?
        How can your kind of spirit be deceived?
MEPH.: Observe! The lines are poorly drawn;
        That one, the angle pointing outward,
        Is, you see, a little *open* . . .

90

Although the important question of rhythm and metre cannot be dealt with here at any length, a few outstanding features will be pointed out. Bartók's rhythm is governed by as strict laws as has been shown to rule his form and harmony. The *circular* character of Movement I of the *Sonata for Two Pianos and Percussion* is in no small degree due to the "absolute" odd metre, 3 times 3 eighths, while the Finale owes its static character to its "absolute" even metre, 2 times 2 eighths. In Movement II, even and odd bars are intentionally alternated.

(Bartók was very much interested in the potentialities of "even" and "odd" metres. In the *Second Piano Concerto*, Mov. II of *Music*, *Violin Concerto*, *Divertimento*, *Mikrokosmos No. 137*, themes presented in even-metred bars return in odd rhythms, or vice versa.)

The rhythms with a "strong" ending in Movement I have counterparts with "weak" endings in the Finale (see Fig. 87).

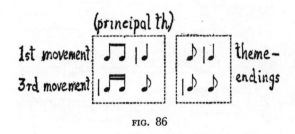

FIG. 86

Consequently the themes of Movement I constitute a *closed*, and those of the Finale an *open* form.

But the polar principle prevails also *within* the even and odd metres: "+ — +" and "— + —" units are periodically alternating in the odd-metred themes, while an alternation of "+ — + —" and "— + — +" units provide the rhythmic pattern of the even-metred tunes.

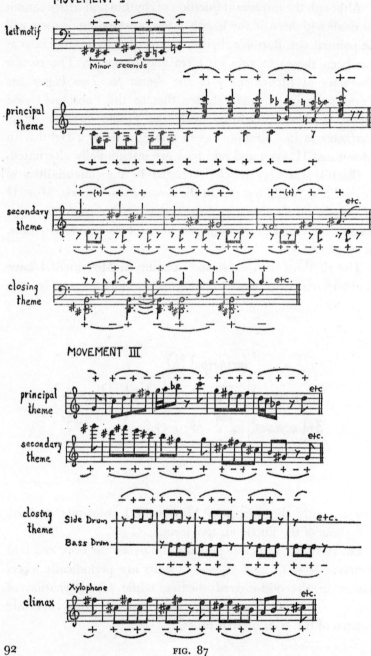

FIG. 87

That is why we feel the following idioms to be so revealing of Bartók.

FIG. 88

As a final example, let us compare the opening and closing bars of the *Sonata for Two Pianos and Percussion*.

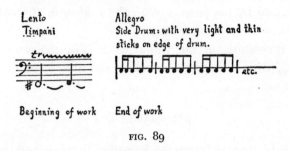

Beginning of work · End of work

FIG. 89

The opening bar gives the impression of descent, as it were, into a well "which is immensely deep, or should we say, has no bottom at all" (Thomas Mann). The low shivering sounds of the timpani really seem to emanate from the negative pole of life, from a phase of preconciousness—the key of which is F♯, the lowest point in the circle of fifths.

Towards the close of the work, the "filliped" cymbal sounded with the nail and the light sticks dancing on the *rim* of the side-drum, produce ostinatos which gambol joyfully over the work, with "slender ankles" on the paths of *light*: in C major, the highest point in the circle of fifths, and counterpole of F♯.

In this way the extreme points of the composition may be regarded as negative and positive poles so that the analogy of a magnetic field offers itself, a current being developed between two opposite poles. The Lento—with its utterly *inarticulated* flow—is represented by the lowest, the Allegro—with its *articulated* rhythm—by the highest drum effect. On the one side a linear, on the other, a rhythmic-spatial element.

Nevertheless, the most interesting circumstance is that the dimensions of the *complete* work were not accidental: it reflects the unity of the correlated principles of the closed *circle* and open *symmetry*. The symbol of the circle is π, while the latter can be expressed by the powers of 2 ($2^2=4$, $4^2=16$, $16^2=256$; the next power is already too large).

The time-value of the whole work (the above-mentioned 6432 eighths) is 804 whole notes, and this is precisely the product of:

$$16^2\pi = 256\pi = 804$$

It can be deduced from the foregoing that one and the same regularity is established throughout many different dimensions of the work, through form, key, harmony, proportions, rhythm, dynamics, colour, etc.

Considering the date (1937) and other particulars, one may risk the supposition that Bartók probably intended the *Sonata for Two Pianos and Percussion* to be a crowning piece: the Makrokosmos of the Mikrokosmos (1926–37).

What role did Bartók's art play in the music of our century? His chromatic system has its roots in Eastern folk music and in pentatony; his acoustic system he owed to Western harmonic thinking. He himself admitted his indebtedness to folk music and the French impressionists as the two most descisive influences on his art.*

* "The two roots of our art originates in folk music and the new French music," wrote Bartók ("Zoltán Kodály": 1921).

This declaration deserves attention for it is well known that he rarely, if ever, committed himself on his own compositions—though he liked to emphasize their relation to folklore, mainly with the intention of propagating *folk* music. "Let my music speak for itself, I lay no claim to any explanation of my works!"

Should his position in music be summed up in a single sentence it might run as follows: Bartók achieved something that no-one had before his time, the symbolic handshake between East and West: a synthesis of the music of Orient and Occident.

*

This essay is the introductory part of the author's book, "Bartók's Style" published in Hungarian in 1953. A following chapter tackles the "dramatic" principles of Bartók's music, especially of his instrumental works. We must not forget that Bartók is, in fact, a dramatic temperament, as all creative genius in whose character the bents for logic and heroism, are united.

Appendix I

Referring to the *Sonata for Two Pianos and Percussion,* it is of interest to point out a few particulars of Movement I. In bs. 235–247 we again notice the two-fold affinity of the axis; on the one hand the G♯ ostinato running through the part and the D counterpole, and on the other hand the constricting funnel-shaped motivic progressions, wedged in the D–G♯ principal branch and later in the F–B secondary branch.

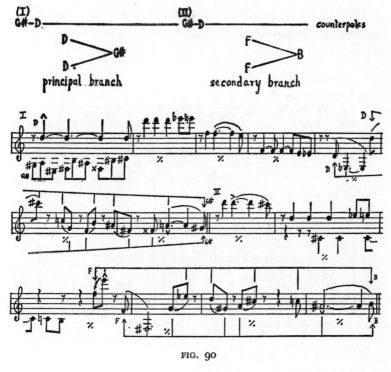

FIG. 90

The four sections of the secondary theme in the recapitulation (bs. 292–330) are based on the four poles of the tonic axis so that their outer and inner parts, respectively, correspond with each other in their pole-counterpole relations.

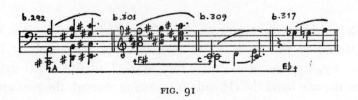

FIG. 91

The axis construction of the coda is equally unambiguous (bs. 417–431). In accordance with the polar scheme the augmented principal theme appears in E♭, then in A, and finally in E♭ + A, over the disjointed E♭–G♭–A–C major-minor (*gamma*) accompaniment chords.

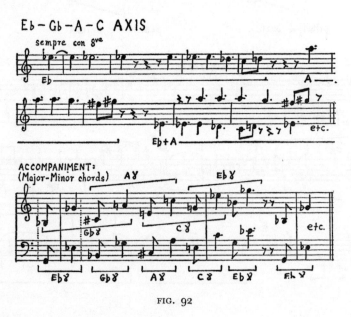

FIG. 92

The development in Movement II of *Music for Strings, Percussion and Celesta* presents an exemplary axis construction:

FIG. 93

The appearance of the Eb–F♯–A–C is always accentuated by the bass drum. The accompaniment, which remains unchanged throughout, stresses the A and Eb counterpoles (*beta* chords):

FIG. 94

It is evident both from the accompaniment and the dynamics that the E♭–A polarity forms the backbone of the structure.

And finally Fig. 95 gives some strongly marked axis melodies.

FIG. 95

Appendix II

A few examples are given to illustrate the interrelations expounded in connection with Fig. 13.

The order of keys of the *First Rondo* is as follows: C tonic, E dominant, A♭ subdominant and C tonic.

Movement I of the *Concerto* is subdivided by the five-fold recurrence of the principal theme:

F tonic (exposition)   b. 76
D♮ subdominant (first part of development) b. 231
A dominant (second part of development)   b. 313
F tonic (recapitulation)   b. 386
F tonic (coda)   b. 488

A similar arrangement is to be seen in Movement I of *Sonata for Two Pianos and Percussion:*

C tonic (exposition)   b. 32
E dominant (first part of development)   b. 161, 195
G♯ subdominant (second part of development) b. 232
C tonic (recapitulation)   b. 274

In the third example of page 45 these relations are: D–A♯–F♯.

The principal theme in Movement II of *Music for Strings, Percussion and Celesta* is particularly cogent, because here we find the cupola-structure and tonic–tonic–dominant–tonic construction of the new-type Hungarian folk songs. The tonic is represented by the C–F♯ counterpoles, the dominant by E–B♭ counterpoles (not by G). The second entry of the tonic provides the exact "tonal answer" of the C–F♯ axis: G–C tones change into C–G and C♯–F♯ into F♯–C♯.

FIG. 96

A similar association of dominant and tonic is evident in bs. 171–178 of Movement I of the *Divertimento*; the E♭–A dominant counterpoles correspond to the F–B tonic counterpoles:

FIG. 97

or at the recapitulation:

FIG. 98

The lower major second degree (e.g. B♭ in C tonality) might justifiably be called the "bartókean dominant" owing to its frequent occurrence in his music:

FIG. 99

which can again be explained by the regularities dealt with above.

The opening bars of the *Miraculous Mandarin* illustrate how the tonic and subdominant are linked; the D♯ tonic swings towards the subdominant F and B counterpoles:

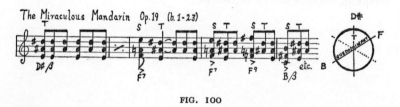

FIG. 100

It is interesting to note that, in Bartók's music, the three functions play a symbolic role too, particularly in his stage works. In *Bluebeard's Castle* this sign-language always goes hand in hand with the plot and contents of the drama. The sub-dominant has a negative meaning being reserved for the expression of fever and passion. All positive movements start with the dominant. The static pillars of the opera and the points of rest are based on the tonic.

The downward pull of the action in the *Miraculous Mandarin* is also expressed by the functional relations. The dominant start of the pantomime (in G) reflects the throbbing excitement of life, whereas the subdominant end of the work (in F) depicts the death of the Mandarin. The intermediate scenes—nearly half of the music—especially where the Mandarin satisfies his desire, are written in the tonic C.

Beginning	Climax	End
G	C	F
DOMINANT	TONIC	SUBDOMINANT

The succession of scenes follows the same *descending* order, a triple descent from the dominant heights to the subdominant depths, as if expressing the idea that the work moves towards a "fateful" abyss:

DOMINANT	TONIC	SUBDOMINANT
1. Visitor (Old Gallant)——→2.	Visitor (Youth)——→3.	Visitor (Mandarin)
1. Waltz——————→2.	Waltz————→	Pursuit
1. Murder ————→2.	Murder ————→3.	Murder

It is for this reason that the scenes, situated one below the other on the above plan, are *variants*—developed from the same material; e.g. the music of the First Murder originates in the basic chord of the First Visitor (Old Gallant):

107

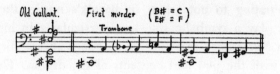

FIG. 101

In the plot of the *Wooden Prince* all this is inversely true. The
scenes follow an *ascending* line, incessantly going up the
T–D–S–T grades:

EXPOSITION	Prelude	TONIC
	Princess	DOMINANT
	Prince	SUBDOMINANT
	Forest	TONIC
	Stream	DOMINANT
	Making of the doll	SUBDOMINANT
	Dance of the Wooden Prince	TONIC
MIDDLE PART	1. Scene (No. 120)	TONIC
	2. Scene (No. 128)	DOMINANT
	3. Scene (No. 132)	SUBDOMINANT
	Conclusion	TONIC
RECAPITULATION =	end of exposition	TONIC
	Wooden Prince (No. 149)	DOMINANT
	Princess and the Stream	SUBDOMINANT
	Denouement	TONIC

For example, here follows the axis structure of the first
scene—Dance of the Princess:*

* A detailed analysis of the work was published in the author's "Bartók's
Dramaturgy": Stage works and Cantata Profana (Editio Musica Budapest,
1964).

108

FIG. 102

Appendix III

An exact golden section can only be constructed geometrically—
it cannot be obtained mathematically, i.e. by means of rational
numbers. The key-number of the GS is irrational (similar to π).

Here is an example of the "Eudoxus" construction, with
square and semi-circle.

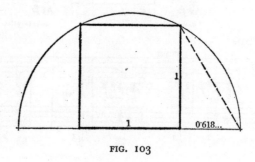

FIG. 103

and another based on the Pythagorean proportion.

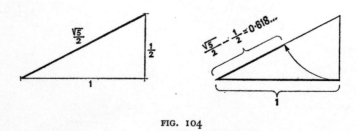

FIG. 104

The hypotenuse (1) of the Kepler triangle subtends a "golden angle" to the shorter perpendicular (0.618 . . .): 51° 49′ 38″ . . .

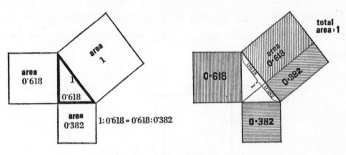

FIG. 105

and a chain of golden sections can be brought about as follows:

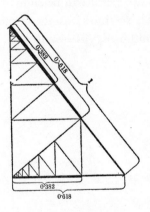

FIG. 106

The members of the GS chain can be obtained by subtraction Thus the GS of 1 is *0·618*, that of the latter: $1 - 0·618 = 0·382$, etc: $0·618 = 0·382 = 0·236$; $0·382 - 0·236 = 0·146$, etc. But the *same* GS chain can also be obtained by involution: $0·618^1 = 0·618$; $0·618^2 = 0·382$; $0·618^3 = 0·236$; $0·618^4 = 0·146$, etc.

The sin and cotan curves meet in one definite point, and precisely in the *golden angle*. The value pertaining to it is: $\sqrt{0·618 \ldots}$

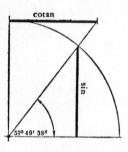

FIG. 107

With the aid of compasses it can be shown that the radius goes 6 times, while its GS 10 times into the circumference of a circle. The Cheops Pyramid in Egypt reveals the following structure:*

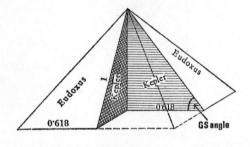

FIG. 108

and so its sloping sides subtend a golden angle.

* After K. Kleppisch and E. Bindel.

The dynamic quality of the Parthenon in Athens owes much to its GS dimensions, and that is why we feel the building soaring upwards, as it were.*

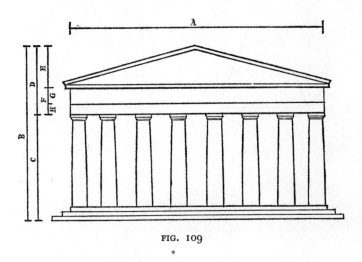

FIG. 109

*

While Gothic architecture favoured angles of 45°, Renaissance art, following the Greek models, showed a predilection for the golden angle. The circle had been given a "heavenly" symbolism, while the square an "earthly" one. Because the Gothic concept subjected earthly affairs to heavenly concerns it forced the square to find a place *within* the circumference of the circle. In contrast to this matters of heaven and earth had an equilibrium in Greek and Renaissance art, therefore, in

* After Zeising.

geometric terms, the circle was coupled with an isoperimetric square. Hence the triangle no more subtended an angle of 45°, but rather the golden angle:

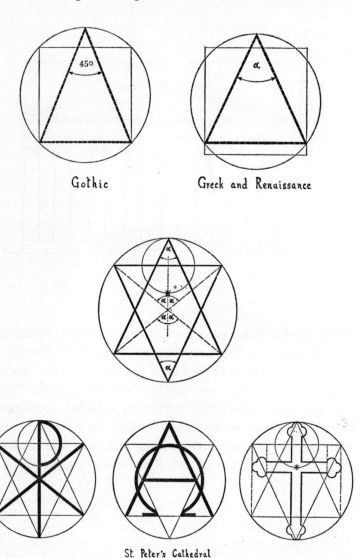

Gothic

Greek and Renaissance

St. Peter's Cathedral

FIG. 110

and the ratios between the three circles in the above letter-symbols show GS relations.*

Zeising derived GS from the proportions of the human body, and held the Belvedere Apollo as the perfect embodiment of it.

Eisenstein planned his film, "Potemkin", in such a way that he placed points of "perfect inactivity" in the negative golden section of each act and those of "highest activity" in the positive sections.

According to Einstein, GS provides a ratio which opposes the bad and facilitates the development of what is good.

"No elements can be properly joined without the aid of a third one, for the two can only be united by the mediation of a link; but of all the links that one is most beautiful which makes a complete whole of itself and of the elements united by it."

Plato: Timaeus.

---

* Cf. Otto Schubert: Gesetz der Baukunst (Seemann—Leipzig 1954).